No Excuse to Lose

Formally dressed in a blazer for the occasion, Dennis Conner awaits
a start in the 1975 Congressional Cup, which he won. *(Photo by John
Rousmaniere.)*

No Excuse to Lose

Winning Yacht Races with Dennis Conner

as told to John Rousmaniere

W W Norton & Company
New York • London

First published as a Norton paperback 1987
Library of Congress Cataloging in Publication Data
Conner, Dennis.
No excuse to lose.
1. Conner, Dennis. 2. Sailors—United States—
Biography. 3. Yacht racing. I. Rousmaniere, John.
II. Title.
GV812.5.C66A36 1978   623.88'092'4 [B]   78-8110

ISBN 0-393-30432-9

W. W. Norton & Company, Inc., 500 Fifth Avenue, New York, N.Y. 10110
W. W. Norton & Company Ltd., 37 Great Russell Street, London WC1B 3NU
2 3 4 5 6 7 8 9 0

Contents

Illustrations   7

Authors' Prefaces   9

Part I: Before the Big Time

    CHAPTER 1   A Sailing Childhood   15

            2   Stars and Congressional Cups   24

Part II: The America's Cup

            3   The Long Summer in *Mariner*   39

            4   Joining *Courageous*   53

            5   Winning the Cup   66

Part III: Ocean Racing

            6   Preparing a Boat   83

            7   The 1975 SORC   96

            8   The Admiral's Cup   105

            9   *High Roler* in 1977   114

6   *Contents*

Part IV: One-Design Racing

10   How to Win a Championship   *131*

11   The Olympic Trials   *146*

12   Bronze Medal at Kingston   *157*

Part V: "No Excuse to Lose"

13   The Heavies—North, Turner,
     Hood, and Melges   *171*

14   Why I Do It   *182*

Illustrations

PLATES

Dennis Conner in the 1975 Congressional
  Cup   *frontispiece*
Bill Buchan   26
Match Racing, 1975 Congressional Cup   29
Mariner, 1974 final trials   54
Below deck in *Courageous*   60
A New 12-Meter, *Independence*   61
Second America's Cup race, foul start   74
Second America's Cup race, foul start   75
Fourth America's Cup race start: *Courageous*
  and *Southern Cross*   77
Doug Peterson and Carl Eichenlaub at the 1977
  SORC   86
High Roler: plans for interior and deck   89
1975 SORC: Conner in *Stinger*   103
High Roler, Bill Power steering   116
High Roler, Conner steering   117
High Roler, a racing boat   124
High Roler, Nassau Cup Race   126

A Tempest start at Kingston   *161*
1976 Olympics—Conner in the fifth race   *164*
Albrechtson and Hansson, gold medal winners   *167*
Lowell North, Rich du Moulin, and John
Marshall on *Enterprise*   *172*
Ted Turner   *176*
Ted Hood at a tune-up sail   *178*
Buddy Melges—"sailing hero"   *180*
The victor . . . 1975 SORC   *187*

FIGURES

1. Pre-start maneuvers   *32*
2. Pre-start maneuvers   *33*
3. Pre-start maneuvers   *33*
4. Protecting the right   *35*
5. Blanketing the competition   *155*

MAPS

1977 SORC

1. St. Petersburg—Boca Grande   *120*
2. St. Petersburg—Ft. Lauderdale   *120*
3. Ocean Triangle   *121*
4. Lipton Cup   *121*
5. Miami—Nassau   *122*
6. Nassau Cup   *122*

AUTHORS' PREFACES

ON SEPTEMBER 10, 1974, I was a thirty-one-year-old San Diego drapery maker who had won a few sailboat races and who was feeling a little sick to his stomach. I was in a boat, but since it was a perfectly calm day in the Atlantic Ocean off Newport, Rhode Island, I was not seasick. Rather, I was thinking about what I would have to do in the next few minutes: steer a 12-Meter yacht in defence of the America's Cup at the start of a race against a highly-touted challenger.

All my life, the America's Cup had been so distant it had seemed surreal. Something I had only read about in *Yachting* magazine. The pinnacle of competitive sailing. A regatta the Eastern Establishment held every three or four years. America's Cup skippers like Harold Vanderbilt, Briggs Cunningham, Bus Mosbacher, and Bob Bavier were my childhood heroes. All of a sudden I realized, "It's just me, Dennis Conner from San Diego, steering this 12-Meter called *Courageous*, with the great Ted Hood standing right here next to me." It was a blow for the common people, when you think about it.

9

Five years earlier, I had never even owned my own boat. Three years earlier, I had accomplished what I had always thought was the second greatest thing in yacht racing—winning a Star Class World Championship. Two years earlier, I had won a Congressional Cup, beating some of the best match-racers in the United States. But only one month before this September 10, I had been the tactician on *Mariner*, a 12-Meter so slow that she could beat other new Twelves only on protests. I had wanted to get the summer over with so I could take my family back home to Southern California. But I had found my way into this cockpit.

This book is about my life in sailing's big time—in the America's Cup, the Olympics, the SORC, the Admiral's Cup. It is about the people and boats in those great events, but, most importantly, it is about what it takes to win those championships. Since I know very little about how other sailors win races, this book is a kind of autobiography. I hope that, by describing how I have prepared and sailed a boat in a big series, I can pass on some of the things I have learned about winning sailboat races, so please excuse all the "I" and "my" references.

SAN DIEGO, CALIFORNIA   DENNIS CONNER

In this short book there are lessons that will help any competitor—whether a sailor, a soccer player, or a business executive—learn from defeat and make the most of a situation in order to perform at the peak of his or her abilities.

Here is the formula for success that led Dennis Conner to win the America's Cup in 1980, to come within a few seconds of winning it against a vastly superior boat in 1983, and to dramatically retake the Cup in *Stars & Stripes* in Fremantle, Australia, in 1987. These lessons apply as much today as they did in 1978, when *No Excuse to Lose* was first published and when Dennis was one of the fastest rising talents in the world of sailing.

By 1983, Dennis was considered one of the very best racing helmsmen. However, his star dimmed when *Liberty* lost the America's Cup in that year. He painfully bore much of the disappointment of defeat. Now, in a comeback that must seem unbelievable to anybody who does not know him, Dennis is indisputably at the very top of his craft. In many ways, he is still pretty much the same person as when this book was written—a drapery manufacturer from San Diego who wants to be able to look at himself in the mirror and say that he can race sailboats better than anyone else in the world. Today he can say that without any hesitation whatsoever.

This book is based on some thirty hours of tapes of conversation between Dennis and myself, during which he talked frankly about his life, ambitions, strengths, and weaknesses. His and my goal was to produce a personal and instructive book that would tell the reader something about what it takes to do well and to win, not only in sailing but in any endeavor. If the proof is in the pudding, we have succeeded.

STAMFORD, CONNECTICUT   JOHN ROUSMANIERE
FEBRUARY 4, 1987

I

Before the Big Time

CHAPTER *1*

A Sailing Childhood

I WAS brought up in San Diego, where I still live. Since our house was only half a block from the San Diego Yacht Club, I hung around the place the way some kids hang around the local pool parlor. But, unlike many of the families that belonged to the club, my parents were not wealthy. My father made enough money to keep the food on the table, but he couldn't afford a boat and he joined the yacht club long after I did. He and my mother gave me a lot of encouragement when I was a junior member, but there never was enough money around for an eight-hundred-dollar Starlet, a small keelboat that was popular there. Perhaps because I could never own my own boat as a kid, I had a bit of an inferiority complex. But since sailing was one of the few things that I could do really well, and since it was important for me to excel at something, I kept at it, racing in many different types of boats as a crew. I never owned my own boat until I was twenty-seven, in 1970, and I owe a great deal to those years of crewing.

Sailing in a variety of boats, both in ocean and one-design racing, I was able to become really well-rounded in a way that young boat-owners are not. I learned an awful lot about boats. Most important of all, exposure to so many different people taught me something about the kind of character and energy that you need to succeed. By the time that I was able to buy my first boat I was eager and well-prepared to be her skipper. I had not only done a lot of crewing in other boats, but I had also been asked by several owners to organize a crew. I was the skipper of some of these boats and the tactician in others. The owners were men who didn't know much about sailing but who liked to feel young by being around young people. So at a fairly young age—seventeen or eighteen—I had the opportunity to get a bunch of guys together and organize them and keep them happy and working together. I still get a thrill inviting on board a good sailor whom I respect and from feeling that he's part of my team. It makes me feel important, I suppose.

The owner often doesn't get the credit he deserves when he recruits a good crew to race his boat. He is smart to get the good guys to go with him and to keep them happy once they are aboard. I see this now because I want Jon Andron, Gary Wiseman, and the other good men to be eager to help me on my boats. I'm certainly willing to take the credit for recruiting them, so I don't see why an owner who may just not be a very good sailor should be criticized for doing the same thing.

Not only was I lucky in being able to crew at an early age, I was also fortunate enough to grow up in San Diego. Many excellent sailors from my home town have made their mark in international sailing and some have been extremely successful in the boating business, but some of the most talented men are relatively unknown outside Southern California. In the first group are people like Lowell North, who won two Olympic medals and four Star World Championships and sailed *Enterprise* in the 1977 America's Cup trials, and Gerald

Driscoll, who won a Star World Championship and sailed *Intrepid* in the 1974 Cup trials. In the second group are North, again, who runs the international North Sails operation, Doug Peterson, the yacht designer, and Carl Eichenlaub, the boat builder. In the third group are Malin Burnham, who won a Star Worlds when he was seventeen but usually sails locally now, though he sailed with Lowell in *Enterprise*, and Ash Bown.

Ashley Bown owns a forty-foot Owens Cutter called *Carousel*, and during the fifties and sixties she was the boat to beat in San Diego's ocean racing fleet. While ocean racing in San Diego was probably not as good as it was in other parts of the world, it offered us some good competition. Ash Bown was the local hero because he was always very hard to beat. As a kid at the yacht club, one of my very first goals was to go sailing with him. But it seemed that, no matter how successful I was with other boats, I just could not get invited on board *Carousel*. I would run down on the float and help with her docking lines and was a pest around the boat all the time. Finally, when I was twenty-one, Ash asked me to crew for him in the 1964 San Diego to Acapulco Race, and that was the beginning of the big time in ocean racing for me.

On board besides Ash and myself were Malin Burnham, Bud Caldwell, and Jim Reynolds (who later crewed for me in Stars)—all San Diego sailing heavies. There were only five because Ash was really worried about keeping the boat light and knew that for every man we would have to carry gear and food at least equal to his weight. Ash was so weight conscious that he didn't take along the working jib, which was too bad because we ran into a bad Santa Ana storm the first night out and dropped way back under mainsail alone, since we didn't want to risk blowing out the genoas. After a few days, we could tell from the other boats' noon position reports over the radio that we were gaining, even though we were never really sure where we were once out of sight of land. *Carousel* didn't have a speedometer or even a depth sounder, so we had to estimate speed. Nobody on board knew how to use the sextant that Ash had brought along because the rules required it—he just stuck it down in the bilge. We finally decided that we could be wherever we wanted, and Ash would ask us before sending the position whether we wanted to be winning the race or losing it. After a while, the other boats became a little suspicious, so Ash and Malin worked up a little skit. Ash would radio a position and then Malin would grab the microphone from him and yell, "No, you dummy, that's tomorrow's position!" One way or the other, it turned out well. We were only twenty-seven miles off our actual position in an eight-day race, beat all of the larger Class C and B boats to the finish, and won the race with a new corrected time record.

Things were a little different on board *Kialoa II*, a seventy-three-footer that John Kilroy asked me to sail in. Her navigator was an airline test pilot named Jim Waller, and after a while I began to believe that he could walk on water. Jim (as Kilroy is nicknamed) gave me a lot of responsibility on the boat, probably more than I was ready for, and I wasn't about to admit that I didn't know how a real navigator did his job. In a San Nicolas Island race in the mid-sixties, only four people on board weren't seasick, and I was one of the people who was. It was blowing about forty, though it seemed like one hundred at the time. I can still remember how it felt to be steering that big boat from the leeward side with all that water pouring over me, sick as a dog. When we got out to the island, it was really treacherous. There's a reef at the end with a wrecked aircraft carrier sitting on it and a narrow cut that you have to pass through. It was the middle of the night and Waller yelled up, "Okay, let's bear off 30 degrees." I couldn't see a damn thing except for breaking water, so I gave the wheel over to Kilroy—it was his brand-new boat—and he steered her through the passage. I was really impressed with how much Kilroy trusted his navigator. If we had been there in *Carousel* and somebody looking at the chart below had yelled up to Bown to bear off 30 degrees, Ash would have told him to go to hell. It was probably simple, since we were on soundings and could use the depth sounder as well as the RDF and ADF, but I was impressed.

Kialoa II taught me many things because sailing in her exposed me to other people and ways of doing things than those I was used to. She was so big that almost every sail needed special equipment, like coffee grinders and two spinnaker poles for jibes. I don't think, however, that I would run the boat the way that Kilroy did, since he could be pretty harsh, though on a boat that big, you have to move fast to avoid trouble. He used to have a buzzer that he would push whenever we had a major problem on deck. We blew out a spinnaker in the 1965 Transpac so he pushed the buzzer and everybody rushed on deck. Since it was muggy below, many of the crew didn't have any clothes on, which was fine except that we were passing an ocean liner close aboard. The liner started tooting its horn because they probably thought we were putting on a show for them, but the scene must have shocked some of the lady passengers.

Gerald Driscoll, the San Diego boatbuilder and a former Star world champion, was along on that race. I didn't know him at all because he did not do too much distance racing and rarely came around the yacht club. I was a member of a group of sailors who sailed in *Carousel*, led by Ash Bown, who was like a second father to me. I was over at Bown's house every night pumping him about ocean racing secrets, and his wife must have hated me because she would keep saying, "Isn't it about time to go home?"

At the same time that I was doing all this ocean racing, I was quite active in Lightnings, which were sailing then on Mission Bay in north San Diego. I crewed at first for Carl Eichenlaub, who in the early sixties was one of the top three in the class in the world, along with Tom Allen and Stu Anderson. The power in the Lightnings in those days was in the northeast and New Jersey, and it was one of the most competitive classes around.

When I started sailing with Carl, back before the 1964 Acapulco Race, I was just one of a few young guys in San Diego who had shown an interest in racing seriously, but since I had never owned a boat of my own, nobody ever knew how good I really was. I helped Carl win a North American Championship plus a second and a third in other North Americans. More important, I got to travel and see how good Tom Allen and the others really were. I learned several things from sailing with Carl, one of which was how to use the compass and another of which was how to pick windshifts. I had a say in the tactics—at least Carl let me *think* I had a say in the tactics—but Carl had the last vote. He sailed the boat very fast, and we made a good combination.

In the meantime, I was going to San Diego State College —like any young kid not knowing what to do with himself. I had summer jobs in sail lofts, and most of my spare time was spent in boats. Finally, I met a fellow named Alan Raffee. He was in his mid-thirties and owned a carpet store. He liked to sail, and, although he wasn't very experienced, he was enthusiastic and tenacious. I can best describe him as the kind of guy who makes the UCLA football team as a guard even though he weighs only 185 pounds. After every Lightning race, he hounded Carl and me about our tactics and our sail trim and, since I liked people who were interested in sailing, we soon got to be friends. After a while he took me out to lunch and asked me to work for him in his carpet store.

"What would you like to do?" Alan asked.

"I'll do anything. I'll wash the johns; I'll sweep the floors. I'll do anything. I'm your boy," I said.

"Well, how much money would you eventually like to make?" he asked.

"Someday, I'd like to make twenty thousand dollars," I answered, though I had no idea what that meant.

"How much do you think you're worth now? But remember that I could never afford to pay you what you're worth because there wouldn't be anything left for me."

He finally hired me for three hundred dollars a month, which seemed like a lot since the only jobs I'd had were in the summer, making minimum wage sewing cringles into sails at Lowell North's loft. Alan and I are now business partners in San Diego.

I soon began to crew for Alan, which was important because he taught me how hard you have to work to get what you want. Some nights we would be working on the boat's bottom, looking through a microscope to find pin pricks to fill. Today we know that wouldn't make any difference, but in those days we didn't know what made a boat go through the water, and Alan wasn't going to leave anything to chance. Whatever it took to make us go the slightest bit faster—we had it. The best sails, the best hardware. If we had to carry a three-and-a-half-pound anchor and our anchor weighted three pounds nine ounces, Alan would take out a file and file off an ounce of galvanizing. I couldn't understand it because I had been able to do well with Eichenlaub and others without this kind of effort. But here was a guy who, unlike me, had not sailed all his life, and he had to work hard at it because he wanted to do well. I enjoyed this and we were like brothers, even though he was fifteen or sixteen years older than I.

Raffee and another fellow in the Lightning fleet, Marty Gleich, were just alike; they both taught me how important it is not only to work hard at something but to work hard at it all the time. You cannot turn moral fiber on and off like a light. There are certain people that you meet who are tough all the time, and Alan and Marty are that way. They were also fortunate enough to be wealthy, yet they lacked natural sailing talent. But they worked hard at racing, even at the insignificant details. For instance, Marty carried a little notebook around with lists of things to do in it: tighten the starboard turnbuckle, mark the mainsheet, and so on. I had thought all along that you could win simply by being a better sailor, but these guys did not have youth or talent or coordination, and they didn't have a lot of friends who sailed. Yet they tried hard and did well. It taught me a great deal.

Alan eventually had a special Lightning boat built that, while not technically illegal, did take every possible advantage of the rules. The hull was very light, and we brought it to the required minimum weight with forty-five-pound teak covers for the pumps under the seats, which did not hurt speed at all. One way or another we got away with it. Things like this may be contrary to the intent of the rules and they usually don't make a damn bit of difference, but sometimes having them gives you a psychological edge.

We qualified for the 1965 Lightning World Championship in Naples, Italy, where we sailed way over our heads and were winning going into the last race. But we didn't have the winning self-image and beat ourselves, so Tom Allen won the series. Still, it was exciting, since I had called all the tactics and trimmed the mainsheet, and it was a positive reinforcement for my ego. It was my sailing ability coupled with Raffee's organizational talents that got us there.

A couple of years later, Alan met Lowell North and they became friends. Lowell was a step ahead of us in international sailing, and he influenced us because he was so successful. Then in his mid-thirties, he was winning in Star boats all around the world and his interest in the Olympics came at a time when nobody in San Diego knew much about winning medals.

We all thought—and Lowell may agree—that the most talented sailor in San Diego was Malin Burnham, who won the 1945 Star Worlds at age seventeen with Lowell, who was fifteen, as his crew. Malin was a natural sailor; he would just take the cover off the boat before the regatta and go sailing— and usually win. It may be that Lowell learned how to work so hard on boats because he found out early that was the only way he could beat Malin. Lowell tells a story about crewing for Malin in the worlds that illustrates this difference in their teenage abilities. Before the crucial last race, Malin asked him which way he thought they should go. Lowell said to go left. Malin said, "That's good enough for me," and went right and won the series. I think that I'm more like Lowell than I'm like Malin, who has more natural talent than we do; we have to work harder on boat preparation.

One reason that Lowell works so hard is that he is a sailmaker. I have had several opportunities to go into the sailmaking business, but I've usually felt that it is important to separate my hobby from my business. I am just not interested in going down to the yacht club and having people come up to me and asking me to look at their sails. But I am interested in making money, and until recently few sailmakers have done really well. I've always wanted to be able to afford everything I wanted. This may be because I couldn't have many things when I was young.

Finally, Lowell and Malin talked Alan Raffee into buying a Star boat, and I was introduced to the Star Class at the 1967 Spring Regatta in New Orleans when Alan and I didn't even know which end went which way on the trailer. Of course, we did not do very well. With time and work, things later improved, though we were not as successful as we had been in the Lightning.

CHAPTER *2*

Stars and Congressional Cups

AFTER CREWING for Raffee in his Star for a couple of years, I decided that it was time to get my own boat. I couldn't afford a Star, so I went into partnership with somebody in a boat in the PC Class. The PCs are cruising-racing boats about thirty-three feet long that have been popular in Southern California for a long time. Since the boat cost $3,400, I figured that this was a reasonable way to get into ownership, at $1,700 for my share, which was all that I could afford. We sailed in a lot of weekend and evening "beer can" races in San Diego, and I eventually won the class national championship in 1970.

Yet I knew all along where the serious competition was—in the Stars. Raffee decided in 1971 that his boat was getting noncompetitive. He wanted a sistership to Lowell North's light redwood Star, so I bought his old boat for about three thousand dollars—a very fair price. My goals that year were modest: all I really hoped to do was to qualify for the World Championship that would be held at Seattle. To qualify, I had to be in the top five at the district championship, and I was very pleasantly surprised to finish second. Having done that, I raised my goal a little to a finish in the top ten at the Worlds. I and my crew, Jim Reynolds, arrived at Seattle feeling pretty confident. Our confidence didn't last very long, however, since the tune-up race showed us that our speed simply wasn't very good. We were well back in the pack—so far back, in fact, that we dropped out early so we wouldn't be one of the last boats to the hoist to be hauled out.

Later, I got to talking with Bill Buchan. Bill is a contractor and boat and sailmaker from Seattle who had won the 1961 and 1970 Star Worlds, so he was somebody whose opinion I valued; I also knew that he wouldn't try to mislead me. He hadn't done very well in the tune-up race, either, and we started talking about sail trim. Finally he asked, "Do you always have so little tension on your main sheet?" I knew that he was honestly curious and was only interested in seeing how I did things, but he got me thinking. Star mainsails always look perfectly trimmed from the deck, with that tall, huge rig twisting off beautifully, but perhaps I was not trimming the sheet hard enough.

There was no wind the first day, so the race was postponed. The next day, I trimmed the sheet a little harder than I had before in light air, had good speed, and went the right way; I got a second and a fifth to give me the series lead. The two race winners had poor finishes in their other races and nobody else was as consistent as I was. I had another fifth in the third race, and from then on just covered Lowell North and stayed out of trouble to win the series.

That Worlds taught me three things. First, the importance of main sheet tension—if it hadn't been for Buchan, we would not have discovered this and brought our speed from mediocre to the top five. Second, consistency pays off—our record was three fifths, a second, and a sixth. And third, never underestimate yourself.

I sold that boat just after the Worlds and bought a new Buchan-built boat, number 5669, with which I won the

Bill Buchan (steering a Star), whom Conner calls one of the top sailors in the United States, gave Conner some advice that helped win the 1971 Star Worlds. *(Photo by Bahamas News Bureau.)*

Spring Series in 1972 at New Orleans and which I then took to the Olympic Trials on San Francisco Bay. Jim and I knew by the start of the trials that we had very good moderate-air speed, but we lost because each race finished in heavy air. It would blow about 15 knots on the first beat, when we would do very well, but it always increased to about 20 on the second beat and 25 to 30 on the last beat, and we would drop back. Buchan and North were both fast, but Allen Holt, from Seattle, had a special heavy-air rig and sail and dominated the series completely. Going into the last race, we were fighting it out with Lowell for third. It blew the hardest of the series in that race and I dropped out because I did not want to damage the boat, which I had just sold, so we finished fourth, with Lowell third and Buchan second. I learned from the trials that I was not all that good in heavy air. This may be because I was brought up in San Diego, where it rarely blows much more than about 15 knots, but, whatever the reason, I'm just not as comfortable in heavy air as I am in light and moderate air.

At about this same time, I started to get involved with match racing. Outside of the America's Cup, the major match race series in North America is the Congressional Cup, a ten-boat round-robin series held every March by the Long Beach Yacht Club, in Long Beach, California. It has almost always been held in Cal 40s, but occasionally it has been held in other popular stock cruising boats. For many years it was little known outside of Southern California. In fact, until Ted Turner won it on his eighth try in 1977, only Southern Californians had won it. In the early years, contestants would bring their own boats, but by the 1970s the club provided boats that were fairly evenly matched.

I first tried out for the series in 1971, when I was beaten in the West Coast eliminations. In 1972 I was second and in 1973 I finally won after a four-way tie for first place. Sailing in *Mariner* kept me out of the 1974 series, but I came back in 1975 to win the cup easily with eight wins and a loss. I did less well in 1976, and then sat out the 1977 series as I prepared my Star.

It was in the Congressonal Cups that I developed the tactics and attitude that helped me win the starting helmsman's berth in *Courageous*. Here, I would like to tell some of what I've learned about this very special type of racing.

Because only two boats are sailing in match racing, you have only two possible questions to ask yourself: "Will I be the aggressor?" or "Will I be the defender?" The choice will depend upon how you view both yourself and the other skipper. Even before you leave the dock, you will have a preconceived notion about your chances at beating your competitor. I know, for instance, that I can leave the dock before a Congressional Cup race being absolutely sure that I can beat Lowell North—though I would not feel that way leaving the dock before a Star race. You have got to psych yourself into feeling that you can beat that other guy and that you can be aggressive and win. If you feel defensive before the start, you will be defensive during the maneuvering—and defensiveness wins very few match-race starts. From that point on, you have got to live up to your aggressive self-image.

Attitude is not everything, of course. Any successful tactic or technique that normally gives you a small advantage in fleet racing will, in match racing, give you a large advantage since it is so hard to catch a leading boat. You must know the rules and be willing to use them to make split-second decisions in order to stay between your competitor and the starting line. You must have an excellent sense of timing. You must have good depth perception, so you can accurately tell whether, for instance, your boat's bow will clear the other boat's stern when you bear off. And you

Match racing requires perfect crew work. Here, despite a huge lead over their competitor, Conner's crew has the spinnaker half-way up in their Cal 40 before she has cleared the mark in the 1975 Congressional Cup. *(Photo by John Rousmaniere.)*

must have a good sense of when your boat is going well or has steerage way.

Here are three tricks that, I am certain, only a handful of successful sailors know about match-race starts. If you use any one of them properly, I almost guarantee that you will get at least a neutral start, and probably the best start.

First, at the ten-minute gun, the two boats approach each other from either end of the line. The ends are usually chosen by a coin toss. You hope that you are approaching on port tack from the port end, so that you will have right-of-way on starboard after the first maneuver. If you are on port, try to pass to leeward of the other boat. Just after clearing his stern, yell, "Ready about," and head up as though you are tacking to get on his stern—but then jibe instead. It is vital that the circling be in a clockwise direction, for reasons that I'll explain in a moment.

The other crew might fall for the fake tack and then jibe to try to get on your stern, but they will end up on port to your starboard tack and you will be in control, if you have jibed well. The idea here is for you to sieze the initiative so that you are in the controlling position. Eventually, you want to be between him and the starting line. The defense against this fake tack/jibe maneuver is for the starboard tack boat to try to pass to leeward of you. Coming from the starboard end of the line, he will head low. You, of course, should head even lower.

The second trick is when you jibe, try to keep your boat going just as fast as possible so that you come out of the jibe with right-of-way on starboard tack with a lot of headway. The way to do this is not to make perfect circles but to trace an egg-shaped, oblong course. Bear off slowly on port tack into the jibe to keep moving fast, jibe quickly and come up hard to close-hauled on starboard (this is where good crew work is vital). The other boat will almost always be surprised by your speed and might have trouble avoiding you. In the 1976 Congressional Cup, I did this in our race against the eventual winner, Dick Deaver. Dick was moving very slowly after tacking to port and could not avoid me as I came back to him close-hauled and rapidly. We had to alter course and protested him. The rules do not permit the right-of-way boat to "hunt down" the other boat by altering her course constantly.

A third trick is to keep sailing between the laylines of the starting marks. If you let the other boat force you outside of those laylines, only one of you will get a good start. Try to do all your circling in the triangle bounded by the laylines and the starting line itself. If the other guy circles better than you do, just sit in the middle of the triangle, luffing. Luffing on starboard tack with little headway will force the other boat to choose whether to luff to leeward or to windward of you. If he sits to leeward, he will try to pinch up under you to make it hard for you to get your boat going as the start approaches. But this won't work if you know your boat and her characteristics. The most basic concern if you are to windward is to make sure that you don't fall down on the other guy and foul him.

When it comes time to get going, both boats will get way on, the leeward boat will go for the port end of the line and the windward boat will tack and go for the starboard end— and the start will be even, unless one end or one side of the course is favored. The start means almost everything in a match race, and, unless the lead boat screws up or is slow, it is hard for him to lose the race. There are, of course, a variety of ways in which the leader can screw up.

First, he could let the trailing boat go off, uncovered, to the favored side of the course. At both Newport, Rhode Island, and Long Beach, California, where the America's Cup and the Congressional Cup are sailed, the prevailing westerlies veer (shift clockwise) as the afternoon wears on. This favors the right-hand side of the course, so the leader should always protect the right. By this, I mean that he should not allow the other boat to get her bow out in front of his boat's when they

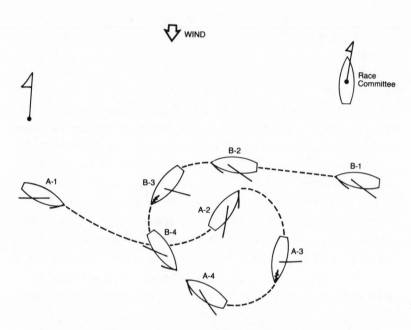

FIGURE 1. Why it is an advantage to have the port end of the starting line in a match race: Boat *A* sails to leeward of Boat *B* and then heads up (*A–2*), faking a tack to get on *B*'s stern. As *B* bears off (to get on *A*'s stern), *A* jibes (*A–3*) and comes up hard on starboard tack (*A–4*), catching *B* on port tack. *B*'s defense would be to not let *A* get to leeward of him by heading below *A* as they approach each other the first time.

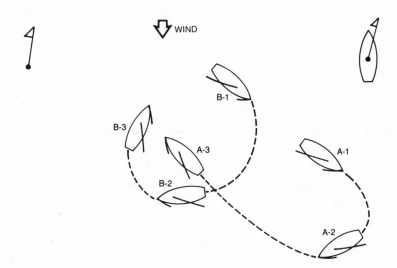

FIGURE 2. Although neither boat has an advantage at *A–1*, *B–1*, *A* is able to starboard-tack *B* at *A–3*, *B–3* because she is able to keep her speed up through the jibe while *B* loses speed in her tight circle. At *B–2*, *B* should realize what is upcoming and not tack to port.

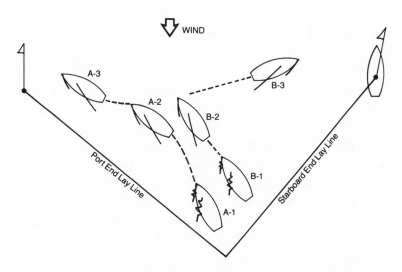

FIGURE 3. The best way to ensure at least an equal start is to stay between the laylines to either end of the line, never letting the other boat drive you outside the laylines. Here, *A* and *B* luff on starboard tack until a minute or so before the starting gun, when they trim sails, bear off to gain speed, and start at either end of the line in clear air. This was how *Courageous* and *Southern Cross* started the first race of the 1974 America's Cup, with *Courageous* in *A*'s position.

are on port tack, allowing the other guy to gain more in headers. The leader should always try to force the other boat back onto starboard tack. This means a tight cover on port tack, sitting on his wind and making him tack, and a loose cover on starboard tack, dead abeam of the other boat. (In any case, a boat sailing closer than 45 degrees to the wind—as a Cal 40 does in moderate air and a 12-Meter does all the time —cannot sit on another boat's wind on both tacks.) Make it easy for the other guy to go the wrong way; make it hard for him to go the right way. Of course, you should not turn down an opportunity to cover your opponent with your wind shadow on the last tack to the mark, as long as you have called the layline correctly.

If you are behind, you should try to make the race as long as possible in order to increase your chances of gaining. This means tacking and jibing duels on the beats and runs. In tacking duels, when you keep tacking time after time after time, do not make the mistake of waiting to get moving before starting to tack again. If you do, the lead boat can get moving, too, and you haven't gained anything. Always try to get him going slower than you are, because, even if you're going only 3 knots, you as the aggressor can take the initiative and gain when he's going 2.8 knots. While you are tacking, keep an eye on the compass; a wind shift might have helped you and you may want to stay on one tack for a while. This is where an alert tactician can help you. Of course, if you are ahead be alert to shifts, too, but never let your opponent go. *Southern Cross* might have beaten us in *Courageous* in the second race of the 1974 America's Cup if her crew had followed this basic match-racing rule. With a good lead, however, don't tempt fate by being suckered into a tacking duel—a nice, loose cover will do.

The runs in match races are as fascinating as the beats, since the trailing boat can attack and lengthen the race and since there is often a "right" side of the course, just as on the beat. At Long Beach, it generally pays to get onto port tack

FIGURE 4. "Protecting the right." Here, *A* keeps *B* in her wind shadow when on port tack to discourage *B* from sailing to the favored right-hand side of the course. Only on the last short tack to the weather mark does *A* blanket *B* on starboard tack. *A* jibes immediately upon rounding the mark to sail toward the favored side.

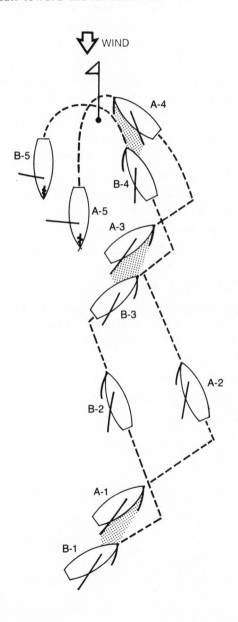

as soon as possible, partly in order to assure gaining the inside position at the leeward mark, and partly to sail toward the favored side of the course (the right-hand side upwind and the left-hand side downwind).

On the run, unlike the beat, the trailing boat can sit on the lead boat's wind. This can be done by jibing and sailing across the lead boat's wake so that when the lead boat jibes to stay between the competition and the mark, her wind is affected. The trailing boat's jibing angle has to be very sharp, even in moderate and fresh air, because her wind shadow has to be "aimed" not at the lead boat but at a spot just *ahead* of the lead boat, into which she will sail. (The wind shadow has to be "aimed" upwind as well; use the masthead fly as your "rifle".) Once the lead boat has jibed and the wind shadow is properly positioned, the trailing boat can bear off again. Ted Turner is especially good at this tactic.

If you are ahead on the run, don't panic; try to jibe before the trailing boat does so you can protect both your position and your clear air and can speed up the race. You don't have to be too defensive when you are in the lead.

Very few good sailors do much match racing at all, so the people most experienced at it always seem to win. By the start of the 1974 America's Cup summer, I had sailed only about thirty match races but I would guess that I had more experience than 90 percent of the top sailors in the United States. If you really want to get good at it, do as much match racing as you possibly can.

II

The America's Cup

CHAPTER *3*

The Long Summer
in Mariner

IN SEPTEMBER, 1973, I received a telephone call from Ted Turner. I knew that he was involved with a new 12-Meter that would be a contender for the 1974 America's Cup defense and I was not surprised when he asked me to sail in the boat. I responded by asking what my job would be and who else would be aboard. Turner was pretty vague about my responsibilities, saying only, "I'd like you to work in the cockpit."

In the cockpit of a Twelve are a helmsman, a navigator, and another couple of men who are responsible for sail trim and sail selection and for advising the helmsman on tactics. The tactician may also be the relief helmsman. Turner said he was going to be skipper and that Rich du Moulin, a Long Island Sound sailor with a lot of ocean racing experience, would be navigator—not that I knew much about navigating anyway. Turner also told me that Robbie Doyle would be on board. Doyle was from Marblehead, where he worked for Ted Hood, the sailmaker who then dominated the 12-Meter business. Then in his mid-twenties, Doyle had put together

39

a good record in small boats, having won two Sears Cups for the North American junior sailing championship and having been an alternate on the 1968 Olympic yachting team. Moreover, he had often sailed with Turner in his ocean racing boats, so I knew that he would have an important position in the Twelve.

My role in the boat's pecking order was important to me for two good reasons. First, I did not want to devote most of the spring and all of the summer of 1974, three thousand miles away from my home and work, unless I could be a valuable asset to the crew. Second, I knew that one good way to get to be skipper of a 12-Meter in an America's Cup year is to have been a tactician and alternate helmsman in a boat in the year of the previous challenge. By being a good number two man, you can persuade the wealthy people who come back year after year to finance these one-and-a-half-million-dollar yachts that you are a good, safe bet as skipper. The hardest thing to do in yacht racing is to be selected as skipper of an America's Cup defender. (And one of the easiest things to do is to win the Cup once you have been selected skipper. United States boats have never lost the Cup in twenty-three matches against foreign challengers in 108 years.) So my plan was to go east to show that I could be a team player, learn about 12-Meters, and aim toward getting invited back the next time as a skipper.

Turner soon after told me that I would be the number two man on the boat, so after talking about the decision with my family and business associates, I accepted the offer. I asked Turner about the organization and schedule for the Twelve, but he knew very little. I eventually called him in November to see if he could ask George Hinman, the syndicate head, about housing in Newport, Rhode Island, where most of the races would be held, and what expenses would be covered. The response was a telegram from Hinman asking all crew members to be at the Mamaroneck, New York, boat yard of

Bob Derecktor, who was to build the Twelve, on the day after Thanksgiving.

That trip east gave me my first exposure to the three people who were to steer, manage, and design the boat that was to be named *Mariner*—Ted Turner, George Hinman, and Brit Chance. First, I flew to Atlanta, Georgia, to spend a day with Turner. Our only contacts had been in some Congressional Cup match-race series, where I beat him regularly, and occasional meetings on the Southern Ocean Racing Conference series of races off Florida and the Bahamas.

Turner was thirty-four years old, but he had put together an amazing sailing record. He had won two SORCs, one in a Cal 40 in 1964, and the other in the converted 12-Meter *American Eagle* in 1970. He had raced in almost every possible ocean race in boats of all sizes—he was then sailing a One Tonner, *Lightnin'*—and, in addition, he had been successful in the Flying Dutchman dinghy class. In ocean racing, he was famous for his ability to get the very best out of his some-times-outdated boats using a steady crew of old friends. His charisma and leadership ability were legendary. That day in Atlanta, I got to know Turner a little better and came to like him a lot. Once you get close to Ted, you've got to appreciate him if only because of his exuberance that sometimes borders on wildness. You don't have to be around him long before you know all about him, because he's so wide open and talkative. I sometimes think that he would have been more at home as a Civil War cavalry leader (Confederate, of course)—I can just see him leading a charge.

The next day, we flew up to New York and drove to Derecktor's yard. Bob Derecktor is also quite colorful, but where Turner is outgoing Bob is a loner, so I wasn't surprised when he barely acknowledged our arrival. Nobody knew where or when the scheduled meeting was going to be held until Ted finally received a message to call George Hinman.

Ted raced to the nearest phone to find out that the meeting was to be held the next day.

Most of the crew, Hinman, Duke Dayton, another syndicate man, and the designer, Brit Chance, met in a diner the next day to talk about the boat. Actually, the Twelve was not owned by a traditional syndicate but by the United States Merchant Marine Academy, at Kings Point, New York. Donors were able to get income tax deductions, which made it easier to raise the huge amount of money needed to build, rig, and sail the boat. This arrangement had been organized by George Hinman, a former New York Yacht Club commodore who had steered Twelves in two previous America's Cup summers. Commodore Hinman, as he was called by everyone (Turner once said that when in doubt about the name of an older man in Newport, you should call him "Commodore" because there were so many of them around), was very different from Turner—much more reserved, very much a member of the Eastern Establishment—but it was he who had chosen as skipper such an anti-establishment guy as Turner. He was to manage the syndicate, an enormous job that included supporting the crew, supervising the planning and maintenance of the boat, keeping track of gear, and raising a lot of money. On top of all this, he planned to be the skipper of another Twelve, *Valiant.* She was a Sparkman & Stephens design that had failed to be selected to defend the Cup in 1970 and that would be both a trial horse for our boat and defense contender in her own right in 1974.

Valiant had been beaten in 1970 by *Intrepid,* the Cup defender also in 1967 and the first of the really modern Twelves, with a separate rudder, a trim tab, and most winches below deck. Originally designed by Sparkman & Stephens (as have all 12-Meter Cup defenders except one), *Intrepid* was altered by a young naval architect named Brit Chance in 1970 and, with Californian Bill Ficker as skipper, she went off to win everything. Hinman had commissioned Chance to design the Kings Point Twelve, and he was at that first crew meeting. Chance had a history of innovative, if not radical, boats, but we couldn't tell that day what the Twelve would look like because he would not show us plans.

It was a strange meeting. Almost all the crew was there, but for Conn Findlay and Legaré Van Ness, who lived in California and Texas, and Derecktor, who couldn't take the time to walk over from his boat yard next door (this amazed me because I had always though the America's Cup was the greatest event in the sailing world). I knew very few of the people, but I did know that almost all of them had sailed with Turner—Robbie Doyle, Richie Boyd, Bunky Helfrich, Marty O'Meara, Doug Fredricks, Billy Adams, and Rich du Moulin. They all knew one another and kidded around a little waiting for the meeting to start. Hinman seemed to be waiting for Turner to run the meeting and Ted was obviously intimidated by the commodore. Finally somebody started talking, and the subject quickly got around to the deck layout of the boat. We could see pretty early that Chance wanted this to be his boat entirely since he was very defensive about some of the recommendations people were making. For example, the foredeck crew wanted to have double hatches forward, on either side, for hoisting and dousing spinnakers, but Chance wanted only one. After some argument, the crew won out. Chance wouldn't tell us anything else about the boat except that she would be smaller than most other Twelves, and it became obvious that he hadn't even shown Turner the plans.

I felt like an outsider at this first crew meeting partly because I didn't know Hinman or Chance and partly because the rest of the crew had sailed thousands of miles with a skipper that I hadn't even been with in a single race. I myself would not organize a crew simply by inviting my friends, as Ted did. I would select the best man for each job whether or not I knew him. (Three years later, for the 1977 Southern Circuit, I chose David Howard to help navigate and call tactics for me in *High Roler,* and I would not have known David Howard if he had walked into my house. This was one of the most important campaigns of my sailing career, and I had to get the best navigator available.)

Another reaction I had to that meeting was that it gave me the distinct impression that Robbie Doyle and not I was going to be the number two man in the boat. There was no animosity, but there was an uneasy feeling between the two of us because neither seemed to know where we stood. Obviously, in his sales pitch to each of us Ted had told the person he was talking to that he would be the number two man. I asked Ted about it and he told me not to worry and tried to soft-pedal my concern. As it eventually turned out, the pecking order on the boat was never confused or a problem, since Robbie was more involved with sail trim and I did tactics.

After the meeting, Turner and I went off with Chance, who had the plans for the boat. I could see that Brit did not want to show us the drawings. The whole thing was so clandestine that it seemed like a CIA operation. I excused myself, half-expecting that Chance would ask me to stay, but all Chance said was, "Okay," so I had to keep on going. I sat in the car while Turner and Chance went over the plans. Chance swore Turner to secrecy and went home. But, of course, Turner came back out to the car and spent the next two hours telling me everything about the boat. In no way is Ted able to keep a secret, and this night he was both a little excited and a little worried because the boat looked a lot different than other Twelves. Still, Brit had convinced him that the design was a real breakthrough.

Turner did not go into all the details, but several months later when *Mariner* was launched we saw a very radical boat. Most 12-Meters are very graceful, with sharp bows, relatively long keels, and sweeping lines back to the stern. *Mariner* had very full, U-shaped bow sections, an extremely short keel, and, oddest of all, a very blunt, truncated after underbody with several steps, like those on a hydroplane. She also had a chine that swept back along the topsides from around amidships to the stern. She certainly was a different-looking boat.

If I hadn't been around Turner, whose excitement is so conta-
gious, I would have felt a little worried, because I have always
felt that people think too much about breakthroughs in sailboats. They should be thinking about doing the very best they
can with the same boats and gear that everybody else has. For
instance, an ocean racer was recently painted with some
"super" covering that the manufacturer said would increase
speed by 8 percent. But, to my way of thinking, if a boat could
be speeded up by 8 percent, somebody would have figured out
how to do it a long time ago.

In January, 1974, Turner, Doyle, four other *Mariner* crew
members, and I won the One Ton North American Championship in one of Ted Hood's *Robin*s off St. Petersburg,
Florida, but I did not hear anything else about the Twelve
until I received another telegram in April, asking me to be at
the launching on May 1. I bought my plane ticket and flew
east, hoping to see a big, red racing machine all ready to go,
flags flying from her rigging.

When I arrived at Derecktor's, I saw that not only was the
boat not in the water (she was to be towed across Long Island
Sound for the commissioning), she was not even near
finished. Even though I had been forewarned by Turner, it
was a real shock to see how different a design she really was.
Turner had missed the launching, but he finally breezed in,
and Chance was there to oversee things.

The next day we all worked hard to get *Mariner* ready for
the commissioning at Kings Point—screwing down floor
boards, bolting down winches, installing the steering wheel.
We finally got the mess cleaned up and a powerboat arrived
to tow us across to Kings Point, on Long Island. It ran us
aground in the mud as we pulled away. We eventually got
unstuck and, as we were towed, we all looked aft to see the
wake, which usually gives you an idea of how a boat is moving
through the water. Usually, the cleaner and quieter the wake
and the smaller the stern wave, the faster the boat. But behind
us was a big, gurgling wave. We were eating and somebody

threw a banana peel overboard. Four or five minutes later someone looked over the side and saw the same banana peel in the same place right behind us, just as though we were towing it and the water it was in. This did not seem at all right.

Later, after the commissioning ceremony, we put on some sails and went sailing. We were under explicit instructions from Commodore Hinman not to sail upwind near *Courageous*, the new Sparkman & Stephens 12-Meter that we thought would be our toughest competitor that summer. But the first time we saw *Courageous*, Turner headed right over to her like she was a magnet. I was about the only one on board who could see what was happening, since almost everybody else was below, and I could tell right away that she was a lot faster than *Mariner*. It was discouraging and I told very few other people what had happened—especially not Commodore Hinman. This gave me an inkling that we weren't quite set up right yet.

We practiced every weekend throughout May, with me flying east from San Diego at my own expense, until our first chance to race in the New York Yacht Club regatta in early June. Even though the yacht club sponsors the selection trials, Commodore Hinman did not want to sail in the two races. The results did not officially affect selection, but they would affect fund-raising. I think we were short of money and Commodore Hinman was afraid that we had everything to lose and nothing to gain if we lost. We had been sailing about equally against him in *Valiant*, but since her stern had been altered to look like ours, it was like the blind leading the blind. We really didn't know where we stood.

We had worked hard on *Mariner*'s boat speed, with Chance following close behind in a powerboat and making comments over a radio. The boat was very hard to steer on a straight course, but Chance kept telling us that Turner wasn't steering properly. Sometimes he would come over in a dinghy and try to show Ted how to steer. At the end of the day, he would have a list of forty or fifty criticisms—our trim was bad or we tacked too fast. Turner accepted this but it was obvious that he was upset since we were doing the best we could. It seemed as though Brit expected perfection.

Somehow, Turner talked Commodore Hinman into letting us sail in the New York Yacht Club regatta, which was held on Long Island Sound. We and *Valiant* had really good starts in the first race, with *Courageous* well to leeward, and we were all very excited. *Courageous* tacked right away to get clear air and we and Commodore Hinman in *Valiant* tacked to cover. As we sailed along on port tack, it looked as though we were outpointing *Courageous* but that she was sailing faster, since the bearing between us and her was changing very slowly in her favor. After a few minutes, she tacked and cleared *Valiant* and I was surprised that we could only just make it across her bow. Obviously, a small amount of bearing change meant a great deal since the boats could point so high (usually within 20 degrees of the apparent wind and 35 degrees of the true wind). Our navigator, Rich du Moulin, had lost the weather mark so I told Turner to tack to cover. We tacked too late, since *Courageous* fetched the mark and we overstood it. We lost to her by three minutes, fifty seconds and laid it off to bad navigation.

My job was to advise Ted on tactics before the start and during the race. He listened to me and followed my advice until the pressure started to build up, and then he did whatever he wanted even if it was the wrong thing. Sometimes he became so nervous that he had a hacking cough and dry heaves.

The next day, we had another good start and tacked to cover *Courageous*. The bearing on her gradually went ahead again, but because we were pointing just as high as she was, if not higher, I thought we were doing pretty well—which once again showed how little I knew. Turner was very nervous and kept asking, "How are we doing?" When she tacked after about five minutes I could see right away that *Courageous* was going to cross us by fifty yards. We tacked to leeward of her, which was the only thing that we could do because we could hope for a header and then tack back and cross her. Again we were pointing, and again she was going over us—at least a knot faster. We were not even in the same ball park, and we lost that race by almost eight minutes.

All this time, Chance was telling Commodore Hinman that we were just bad sailors who were hacking it up, which I had to believe because I knew that Bob Bavier and his crew in *Courageous* were a lot more experienced than we were. Bavier had been skipper of *Constellation* when she won the 1964 America's Cup. None of us in *Mariner* had raced in an up-to-date 12-Meter, although Turner and most of the crew had ocean raced in *American Eagle,* a 1964 design. We didn't even know where the jib leads should go or how hard to trim the sails. So Chance and his ten-page lists were pretty convincing, although they were also not helping our self-confidence. Meanwhile, George Hinman wasn't saying much since he wanted to beat us and win the trials in *Valiant.*

We kept practicing three days a week and finally, in the middle of June, towed *Mariner* up to Newport, Rhode Island, for the early trials. I had a private room in the college where the crew was housed, but I soon had my wife and two young daughters come east to be with me. Commodore Hinman did not want any children in the college, so we had to rent a house in Newport, which was both expensive and inconvenient. In addition, it was difficult getting away from the college because Turner needed constant companionship. We were all very busy since, unlike the other crews, we had no paid hands to maintain *Mariner* and *Valiant* and had to do most of the work ourselves.

To say the least, we were apprehensive about the June trials (the first of three), with very little confidence both in the boat and in ourselves. We won our first race, against *Valiant,* and then came up against *Intrepid* in the second race, in about 15 knots of wind. *Intrepid,* a wooden boat unlike the two new aluminum Twelves, had won the 1967 and 1970 America's Cups under Bus Mosbacher and Bill Ficker. This year, she was owned by the Seattle [Washington] Sailing Foundation, which had commissioned Sparkman & Stephens to update her hull. Olin Stephens had removed all of the underwater modifications that Brit Chance had made to her, and the work was done in San Diego at Gerald Driscoll's yard. Driscoll was also *Intrepid*'s skipper. Even though at this stage I was sure that the trials would come down to *Courageous* and ourselves, I was challenged to be sailing against my old San Diego Star Class rival.

Turner was very aggressive in the maneuvering and won the start by a large margin, with us abeam and well to windward of *Intrepid*. He was incredibly nervous, jumping around and yelling at everybody.

"How are we doing?" he screamed.

I looked at *Intrepid* through my hand-bearing compass.

"They're pointing a little higher," I said.

So Turner yelled to pull in the sails a little more so we could point higher. We were all getting upset because he was yelling so much.

"Pull up my pants!" he screamed, so somebody pulled up his slicker pants, which had fallen down.

"How are we doing now?" he yelled.

I looked through my hand-bearing compass again.

"They're going a little faster," I said.

Nobody said anything, since all I was doing was giving out bad news.

"Now how are we doing?" Turner yelled again.

"They're going higher *and* faster," I said. It was terrible.

I asked du Moulin to look at the polar diagrams and tell us how fast and high we should be sailing. A polar diagram is a chart drawn by the designer that shows a boat's theoretical speed and pointing ability in all wind conditions. I told Turner how fast we should be going.

"We're going a knot faster!" he yelled back.

That only showed us how screwed up we really were.

I said, "They're killing us, sailing right through us. We've got to tack." I wanted to start a tacking duel, which is what we used to do in the Congressional Cup when we got behind. The idea is that if you tack a lot either you might get your own boat going better or the other guy might make a mistake. So we started tacking and they kept gaining. It's hard work to make a lot of tacks, and Turner kept yelling encouragement like, "We'll keep tacking until they drop!"

And, sure enough, *Intrepid* ripped her jib. Guys ran out on her foredeck to put up a new sail and we started yelling, "We're going to get them, we're going to catch them!" Just when we got up even with them, they pulled their new genoa up—and motored away from us just like before to round the weather mark one and one-half minutes ahead. We lost about half a minute on the reaches and *Intrepid* won by two minutes, fifty-two seconds.

We then beat *Valiant,* and *Courageous* came from behind to beat *Intrepid.* The next day, *Courageous* slaughtered us by almost ten minutes and *Intrepid* easily beat *Valiant.*

That set the whole, depressing tone for *Mariner*'s Cup campaign. As Turner said after *Intrepid* passed us so easily in that first race, "It's going to be a long summer." *Courageous* and *Intrepid* beat us by a total of fifteen minutes, twenty-six seconds in the three races we sailed against them, and we had to struggle to beat *Valiant.*

It was obvious that we had to make a change in the boat. The crew was 100 percent in favor of some alteration as was Turner, who at one stage told Chance, "Jesus, Brit, even a turd's tapered at both ends," referring to the squared-off stern. The only guy not for a change was Chance, who blamed Turner and the crew for *Mariner*'s lack of success. The designer and the skipper were hardly speaking to each other by now.

Commodore Hinman believed that something was wrong with the design, too, because he had Chance go into a crash program to redo *Mariner* as early as the second day of the June trials. He pulled both *Mariner* and *Valiant* out before the series even ended and had them towed back to Mamaroneck for alterations. *Valiant* was returned to her original Sparkman & Stephens shape and towed to Newport so we could race her in the July trials, but *Mariner*'s after underbody was completely cut off and replaced with a more conventional design. The cost of all of this was said to be more than $250,000. Ted and I sailed *Valiant* with little success, although we did get ahead of *Intrepid* in one heavy-air race and, as Driscoll started to overhaul us as we approached the finish, Turner gave a sharp luff and there was contact. We won the protest. It turned out to be one of the two wins by either of our boats over *Courageous* or *Intrepid* in the entire summer. Those two boats were having a hard fight with the older *Intrepid* winning a majority of the races, to everybody's surprise.

Meanwhile, Turner was doing a fantastic job of keeping spirits up, showing what kind of leader he really is. It would have been easy for all of us to have become depressed, but his charisma, sense of humor, and determination set an example. It struck me that Ted's personality swings were so extreme. He could be such a confident leader ashore but so hyper and nervous on the boat that he could upset the entire crew by the start of a race. One of the crew was asked by a filmmaker what it felt like to be yelled at so much and he answered that getting angry at Turner may have made him a better crew. I doubt it. It could be that Turner's personality was more suited for ocean racing than it was for day racing. You can't emulate a personality like that—there can be only one Ted Turner— and his winning the 1977 America's Cup showed him at his best, winning in the underdog boat.

After *Mariner* was rebuilt and returned to Newport, I was given the helm of *Valiant*. I had steered *Mariner* very little, and perhaps Commodore Hinman decided that I should be given the opportunity to prove myself. He may have also felt that my replacing him would give him more time to run the campaign, which was what he did best.

One day we in *Valiant* sailed close by *Courageous* and her crew asked us if we wanted to do some starting. We said, "sure," of course, and the *Courageous* people set up a starting line. We really whipped her in half a dozen starts in very light air, where *Valiant* is not at all at her best, and they thanked us and left. Perhaps that news got back to Commodore Hinman, because he soon scheduled a series of short races between *Valiant* and *Mariner*. In the starts, I just slaughtered Turner. Perhaps he was nervous, but it was so bad that in one starting sequence we made him foul us two or three times within five minutes. The next morning, Hinman said that we would have four races, with Turner and I steering each boat twice. Again, I won the starts, but Turner, who sails particularly well on a run, passed me downwind in one race, so we were pretty even for the day.

But the next day, Commodore Hinman offered me the helm of *Mariner* and said I could pick my own crew. In two days the final trials would start, with me at the helm of a new 12-Meter. Turner held a dramatic crew meeting on the pier that morning to tell everybody the news. It put me in an uncomfortable position, but I made three switches in the crew and had Robbie Doyle be my number two man. Turner would sail *Valiant*, and I now was a 12-Meter skipper.

CHAPTER *4*

Joining Courageous

I was a 12-Meter skipper, but not for long—six races in fact. But *Mariner* did much better in those races than she had done all summer, winning three, leading at one stage in two others, and gaining before a breakdown in the sixth.

The very first race of the final trials, we easily beat *Intrepid* in a light-air start. We led to the weather mark, but *Intrepid* caught us in a jibing duel at the end of the first reach and went on to win by two minutes. We were encouraged, partly because we led for so long and partly because losing by two minutes is a lot better than losing by ten minutes. Bob Bavier, in *Courageous,* fouled us at the start of the second race while trying to cross us on port tack, and he was later disqualified from a race that he otherwise won easily. In the third race we beat *Valiant* to make our record two and one, and in the fourth race we beat *Intrepid* again at the start and led her all the way around the triangle before she caught us on the second beat. The series ended with two short races in moderate to fresh winds. Against *Courageous,* we had a fairly even

start and began to gain in a tacking duel when a genoa sheet shackle opened up and they beat us badly. Finally, in the sixth race, Turner in *Valiant* led us all the way around the course but failed to cover at the end, and we won our third race.

Despite our marked improvement, the New York Yacht Club's America's Cup Committee decided that it was time to eliminate both *Mariner* and *Valiant* from the trials so it could concentrate on the problem of selecting a defender between *Intrepid* and *Courageous*, which were very even. That evening as we put the boats away, a launch came up and, with tears in our eyes, we heard Commodore Henry Morgan, the committee's chairman, thank us for our efforts and excuse us from the trials.

I was of course unhappy, but I felt a little relieved. Nobody who hasn't done it knows what it feels like to sail a boat that wins only on protests. It is like going fifteen rounds with Muhammad Ali—after the first two rounds you just don't want any more. *Mariner* had proven herself to be one of the slowest 12-Meters of modern times, sailing against boats, one seven years older, that were gaining close to two minutes on every weather leg. Those six races as her skipper gave me my satisfaction for the summer, and I went out and got drunk with the crew and helped clean up the boat. I really didn't want to stick around to see who would win between *Courageous* and *Intrepid*; I'd had enough; I wanted to go home to San Diego with my wife and daughters and go back to work. But then I received a phone call from the New York Yacht Club's Vice Commodore, Bob McCullough, who was managing *Courageous*, asking me to go with him and watch that day's race. Frankly, I didn't feel like going out because the experience would have only poured salt in my wounds. But I'd always heard that the losing skipper in a Cup trials is supposed to help the winning guy, so I told him that I'd love to go out.

Mariner (rear), with Conner at the helm, leading *Courageous* at the start of a race in the final trials in 1974. *(Photo by John Rousmaniere.)*

We were on one of his syndicate's power boats with Olin Stephens, who had designed both *Courageous* and *Intrepid*, and as we watched the race, McCullough and I talked about what was going on. It was a great day for him since *Courageous* won easily. She had been about equal—and often less than equal —with *Intrepid* all summer, even though she was the newer boat. Bob Bavier, who had been the Cup-winning skipper in 1964, was her skipper and Ted Hood, the sailmaker, had just been made her tactician. Still, they had been having a lot of trouble beating *Intrepid*. When we came ashore, I thanked McCullough for taking me out and expected to go home, but he asked me over to the *Courageous* crew's house for dinner. It seemed to me that they were trying to get to know me a little better.

Dinner with the *Courageous* group was much different than it had been over at *Mariner*'s house. It was more formal, with the meals served by waiters and everybody in jacket and tie. There were wives and girl friends at the table, too, so everybody seemed to be a lot happier, though this might have been because they were winning races. You can hardly imagine the depression that comes when the only races you ever win are on protests.

After dinner, McCullough excused himself and the crew for a meeting. I was pretty impressed by this—a little meeting for the crew to talk over the day's races. We never had crew meetings on *Mariner*. Little did I know that they were talking about asking me to sail in the boat.

Apparently, the vote was split because the crew knew that I would replace Tom O'Brien, who had been trimming the main sheet all summer. They had understandably built up a strong comaraderie over a period of time, so they were thinking that I would kick O'Brien off the boat even though he had been working hard all summer. Some people not connected with the boat later said that the crew was against me because I had gained a reputation for being too aggressive, especially on the starting line. True, I had beaten Bob Bavier in some practice starts and had won most of the starts as *Mariner*'s skipper, but I think the guys just felt badly for Tom. They weren't overconfident about beating *Intrepid* and I'm sure they would have liked to have had my help—but they hated to see one of their friends leave as a result.

In any case, after the meeting McCullough, Bavier, and a couple of syndicate members asked me into the study, and Bavier said that the crew had met and had decided to ask me to sail with them.

I was honestly surprised and said, "I'm flattered."

There was a silence, and I could see that Bavier was a bit uneasy. After a moment, McCullough said, "Not only are we asking you to come aboard *Courageous*, but we want you to steer the boat at the start, too. We want you to start the boat."

I leaned forward with my eyes popping out of my head and said, "Start the boat!" with a little squeak in my voice. I was really excited. After a few moments, I asked if I could steer the boat on the way in from the race the next day to get the feel of her.

McCullough said, "We want you to start the boat tomorrow."

"Tomorrow?" I said, shocked.

"Yes, tomorrow," he said. He then leaned over me—he's very tall and commanding—and he said, "Young man, I don't want you to feel like we're putting any undue pressure on you. I don't want you to feel like you have to dominate them at the start. Just as long as you're comfortably ahead."

So I said, "Thanks very much," and went back to my rented house and told my wife, Judy, the good news. I had a little trouble sleeping that night. Here I was thirty-one years old and about to start a boat I'd never sailed in the final trials for the America's Cup.

The situation was confused in the boat because I would steer at starts, Ted Hood would steer upwind, and Bavier would steer downwind. This was how McCullough wanted it, and he was the boss. He had reorganized the syndicate in

November, 1973, when it looked as though they couldn't raise enough money and they decided not to build a new boat. Bill Ficker, *Intrepid*'s skipper when she won the Cup in 1970, was going to be in charge of the new boat, but when the syndicate collapsed he made so many business commitments for 1974 that he couldn't come back in as skipper when McCullough got things organized again. So Bavier, who had won the Cup once and whom everybody in the syndicate knew and trusted, was chosen.

When the America's Cup summer began, most observers thought that Bavier in *Courageous* and Turner in *Mariner* would fight it out for the right to defend. But, of course, *Mariner* proved to be slow and the seven-year-old *Intrepid* turned out to be at least as good as *Courageous*. Bavier began to lose starts to Gerald Driscoll, and McCullough began to change personnel on the boat. Jack Sutphen was replaced as the tactician by Ted Hood, who was free because a boat he had intended to race in England was stuck in mid-Atlantic on a disabled freighter. And then I came aboard.

Bob Bavier was not very comfortable in this situation— who would have been? Here he was the skipper of his own boat and he wouldn't even start her. Apparently, McCullough thought that I was the best starting helmsman, even though it meant dividing responsibility on the boat.

The next morning we went down to the boat and rigged her, and were towed out to the line. We really didn't talk at all about what I was going to do or what was going to happen. We dropped the tow near the starting line and Bavier told the crew to get the sails up. We sailed around for a while with Bavier at the helm, and then finally at about the time of the warning gun he turned the wheel over to me. It was the first time that I had been at *Courageous*'s helm, but we won the start.

I was surprised at how easy it was to take starts from Driscoll. He would try something different each time, but at almost every start he would give up and we would have him. Each morning we expected an announcement that their tactician, Bill Buchan, like Driscoll and myself a former Star world champion, would take over. Driscoll did win one when he was able to use my aggressiveness against me. He sailed far away from the line with us tailing him and then came back just slowly enough so that we ran out of time and trailed him across the line. The rest of the time, we beat them.

But it wasn't so easy in the races. In the first race, they slowly caught us and eventually got by to win. Then, in a race that was eventually called off because the wind was so light, *Intrepid* sailed over us on a reach because we had the wrong spinnaker up. The leg had started as a broad reach and we were right to have a very light, half-ounce spinnaker up. But when the wind freshened and came ahead, the half-ounce stretched too much. *Intrepid* behind us was carrying a three-quarter-ounce spinnaker, which was the right sail because it stretched less, and she started to move faster, but Bavier wouldn't call for a change even though our navigator, Halsey Herreshoff, kept trying to talk him into it. He finally decided to do it, but too late and *Intrepid* passed us. Even though the race was called off, this indecisiveness was probably the reason why McCullough eventually replaced Bavier with Hood.

I was completely in charge during the start, and Hood and Bavier would work the running backstays. Then I would hand the helm over to Hood and go trim the main sheet. When I left the wheel, I'd feel like I was going back to the dugout after hitting a home run, with everybody patting me on the back and saying, "Nice going." There was no animosity or jealousy because we were doing well at the starts and everybody was pleased. The mainsheet winch in *Courageous* was below so I really couldn't see much, but when I saw things that were obviously wrong, I would tell Halsey about them and he would try to talk Bavier and Hood into correcting them.

This took us up to the Saturday before Labor Day Monday, when the Cup committee had to choose a defender. We and *Intrepid* were tied, 2–2, in the final trials so it was obvious

The new 12-Meters for the 1977 America's Cup had most of their winches and crew on deck. This is Ted Hood's *Independence*, with the mainsheet winch in the foreground, then the genoa sheet coffee grinder handles and the radiused boom vang. *(Photo by John Rousmaniere.)*

Below deck in a 12-Meter (old-style). This is what Conner saw from his mainsheet trimmer's position in *Courageous. (Photo by John Rousmaniere.)*

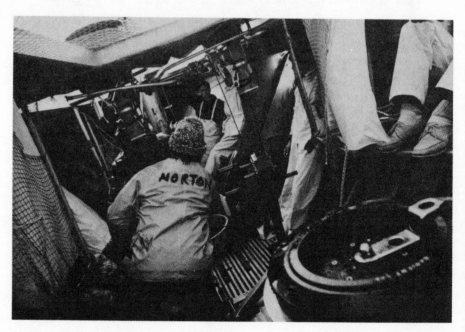

that it was all going to come down to those last races.

Saturday afternoon, McCullough told me that he was to make a change the next day and that I should act surprised —Ted Hood was going to become skipper, Bob Bavier was going to get off the boat, and I was going to be tactician. Bavier was told about it Sunday morning and took it very well. We didn't race that day because it was foggy, but we did go out in the bay for a sail, with Bavier in a powerboat, observing.

What this meant was that we had to win on Monday, September 2, the final day for choosing an American defender. If we had not raced, the Cup Committee would have had a difficult choice between the old boat that had done well all summer, *Intrepid*, and the new one that had had trouble getting going, *Courageous*. As it was, we raced in the strongest wind of the summer—25 or 30 knots with big seas. I was a little scared before the start because we were a bit out of control, and when we pulled sheets in we kept waiting for something to break. Hood said, "What do you think about the start?" And I said that I really was worried because I hadn't sailed Twelves all that much and I wasn't sure what would happen when we began our pre-start circling. Ted and I more or less decided that he should steer, since he was more familiar with Twelves (even though he hadn't steered *Courageous* much longer than I had), and that we should not attack but rather be very conservative before the start. The 12-Meters that we sailed that year were very wet boats, with low freeboard and a lot of deck openings, so there was always a worry about taking too much water below. (After the 1974 series, the rules were changed to require self-bailing cockpits and to limit deck openings, and 12-Meters now look more like ocean racing boats than big, open one-designs that were always full of water whenever it got rough.)

We did no circling with *Intrepid*, and when the boats eventually did come together it was well to leeward of the starting line. Since it was a lot rougher than we had thought, we were not going very fast upwind and we were both late to the start. We were on starboard tack heading for the line and Driscoll, on port, could have crossed us and tacked to cover. But instead, he tacked under us, and we both crossed the line on starboard. At first, it appeared as though they were a little faster, a couple of hundred yards off our leeward bow, but the speed evened out. Normally we figured that at 8 knots, it took us about twelve minutes to get to a layline, so after ten minutes I asked Halsey Herreshoff, "How much farther to the layline?" He said it was about a minute away, and then, a minute later, he said, "We're on it."

Yet there was no reason to tack, since *Intrepid* was even farther along. The more we both overstood the mark, the more distance she would lose after we tacked to port since she would have to fall back into our wake.

I said, "Halsey, are you sure?" Hood never became involved with these conversations about tactics. He just concentrated on steering.

Halsey answered, "We're definitely beyond the layline." So I said, "Ted, we ought to tack." He shrugged his shoulders and said, "Ready about."

Just after we tacked to port, *Intrepid* tacked, and almost immediately her port lower running backstay broke. This meant that they could not control the bend of their mast on port tack and it would have hurt them badly if they were sailing hard on the wind. Since they had overstood, they bore off a little and sailed down into our wake. It turned out that we had both overstood, and we had a forty-two–second lead at the first mark.

It was blowing very hard on the reach and even without a spinnaker, steering was difficult. So after we hooked up the pole and a starcut reaching spinnaker, I told Ted that we should not set the sail unless *Intrepid* set theirs, which we knew would be a special asymmetrical reaching chute. This is an old small-boat tactic. You have everything to lose and very little to gain if you set first when

you're leading in heavy air. If you have bad control problems, you might lose the lead. If the spinnaker works, all
you do is gain a little.

Intrepid set her special spinnaker immediately, so I yelled
to our crew to hoist our starcut. But as soon as I saw what
was happening astern, I told the crew to hold up. *Intrepid's*
spinnaker filled and she heeled way over on her side. The
spinnaker collapsed and *Intrepid* straightened up, but it filled
again and she went way over on her side a second time and
the sail tore into pieces. We sailed a little high so we could
bear off later and set the chute, and by the end of the second
reach we had gained a few seconds.

We covered *Intrepid* up the second beat until I saw that we
were in a big lift, so I told Ted that we should let them go off
on the headed tack. That's a difficult decision—to cover or to
sail the lifted tack—but we were right this time, eventually
were headed 10 degrees, tacked back, and tripled our lead.
Halsey called for a jibe-set onto port tack at the windward
mark and we gained some more, since *Intrepid* did not jibe and
sailed away from the rhumb line for four minutes. It was
blowing so hard and the seas were so rough that we did not
lower the genoa on that run because we were afraid we might
lose it overboard. Both Hood and I steered, one on each
wheel. It was wild sailing, with the boat making great rolls
one way and the other and Hood standing there calmly, not
saying a word.

Our lead was so big that we just covered loosely on the
last beat and won by one minute, forty-seven seconds. After
we finished, all the guys came on deck and we passed
around champagne, congratulating ourselves on how smart
we had been. But if *Intrepid* had not blown the start and if
she hadn't overstood the first mark so badly, it would have
been Gerald Driscoll and Bill Buchan anticipating some
good news from Commodore Morgan, and not Ted Hood
and Dennis Conner. They had sailed *Intrepid* to at least 95

percent of her potential and had almost beaten us who, new to *Courageous*, were getting no more than about 85 percent out of a better boat. With the celebrating over, we now had to look forward to sailing against *Southern Cross*, the Australian 12-Meter that had demolished the French contender in the Challengers' trials.

CHAPTER 5

Winning the Cup

AFTER COURAGEOUS beat *Southern Cross*, 4–0, to win the 1974 America's Cup series, almost everybody seemed to think that it had been a walkover for the Americans. But from my position as starting helmsman and tactician in the winning boat, that definitely was not the case, especially in the first two races. The winning margins in those races were four minutes, fifty-four seconds and one minute, eleven seconds, but the sailing was much closer than those times indicate. *Southern Cross* was a very fast boat that could have won those races if her crew had not made several key mistakes in tactics. Had she won the first two, her impetuous owner, Alan Bond, might not have made the crew and sail changes that literally gave away the third and fourth races.

Bond, a Perth, Australia, land developer in his mid-thirties, seemed to be using the America's Cup campaign primarily as a publicity stunt for his business schemes. Whatever his purposes, he spent an enormous amount of money (some said five million dollars) on the design, construction, rigging, and

maintenance of *Southern Cross.* She was designed by Bob
Miller and Craig Whitworth and built of aluminum on the
east coast of Australia before being trucked across the conti-
nent to Perth. Her sails were made by a loft that Miller and
Whitworth owned. She tuned during the Australian summer
of 1974 against the 1970 challenger, *Gretel II.* When the word
got out that *Gretel II,* which had been very fast and had won
a race in the 1970 series, was regularly being beaten by the
new boat, everybody in the United States began to get worried. (We later discovered that *Gretel II* was not kept in her
peak 1970 condition.)

Southern Cross's skipper was Jim Hardy, a champion
dinghy sailor and *Gretel II*'s helmsman in 1970. Her tactician
some of the time was John Cuneo, the 1972 Olympic gold
medalist in the Dragon Class. They were good and so was the
boat, but unlike the American crews they did not have a
whole summer of serious racing under their belts when the
first race started on September 10. Not until she sailed against
France in the challengers' elimination trials did she really race
in anger, and she was so far superior to the French boat that
even those races were not especially instructive.

If the Australians were still learning as the Cup series
progressed, so were Ted Hood and myself, veterans of only
a few races in *Courageous.* An important decision that we had
to make before the first race was that of sail selection. For the
first time, two American sailmakers were making good 12-
Meter sails. One was Hood himself, who had dominated the
Twelves ever since the first challenge in that class in 1958. But,
this year, North Sails had produced the inventory for *Intrepid,*
in which one of their loft managers, John Marshall, was sailing. *Intrepid*'s early summer success against the newer boat
convinced many people that the North sails were faster than
the Hoods. When the *Courageous* syndicate bought a North
mainsail and some North genoa jibs in August, they seemed
to confirm this impression.

During the final trials and some pre-Cup tuning against

Intrepid, almost everybody came to believe that the North mainsail was superior in light to moderate winds and that a Hood main was better in fresh air. A third main, originally built for *Intrepid* in 1967, was the choice for heavy air, and we used it in the windy final race against *Intrepid.* I felt that we had a little more power with the North sail, which had a tighter leech than the Hood. It was constructed differently, also. Stretch and the resulting distortion of sailcloth is a major problem on boats this large, and John Marshall had not been happy with the stretch characteristics of the 10- and 12-ounce cloth that would normally be used in a Twelve's main. So he sewed together two layers of a 6-ounce cloth that had excellent resistance to stretch to make a two-ply sail. Hood, who makes his own sailcloth, felt that he could control the stretch problem and save weight aloft by using 9.8-ounce cloth in a single ply.

Bob McCullough, the syndicate head, wanted us to use the North sail in light air, even though Hood had built a special light-air main. During a conference on the pier before we left, McCullough said, "We've concluded that the North sail is the one to use up to about 16 knots of wind. Don't you agree, Ted?"

Hood said, "I don't necessarily agree, but you're the boss." Halsey Herreshoff, the navigator, and I thought that this covered the issue, but we were still worried that Ted might want to use his own new sail.

We towed out to the starting line with both sails on board. The wind was quite light. Ted was quiet for a long time, and then he finally said, "Let's get that Hood main up." Halsey and I looked at each other in disbelief. Bob McCullough, on a powerboat nearby, could see what was happening since the Hood cloth was slightly darker than the cloth in the North sail. He called us over the radio we used before the races: "*Escort* to *Courageous.* What's that Hood main doing up?"

I heard him and I turned to Hood and said, "Bob wants to know what we're doing with the Hood main up."

Hood said, "Tell him we're just taking a look at it to see what we can do to improve it." This was two hours before the start of an America's Cup race, when you don't usually spend much time evaluating new sails, but I passed it along to McCullough anyway.

A little later, we were in the starting area surrounded by the huge spectator fleet. McCullough radioed over, *"Escort* to *Courageous.* Okay, there's forty-five minutes to go. Let's get that North main up."

I answered, *"Courageous* to *Escort.* Just a minute."

It seemed like a good idea to be a little more tactful than Bob McCullough had been, so I said to Hood, "Hey, Ted, Bob wants us to consider putting the North main up."

There was a long silence, and then Hood said, "You tell Bob that I'm the skipper and that we're going with what we have up."

So I got on the radio and said, just as fast as I could, *"Courageous* to *Escort.* Tedsayshe'stheskipperandwe'regoing-withwhatwehaveup. *Courageous* out." And I got the hell out of the way of the radio.

This really put Hood on the spot. We might win with his mainsail up, but if we lost he would be personally blamed for letting business interfere with what should have been an objective evaluation of the relative merits of the two sails. It could have ruined his reputation and his career. In any case, though we won, John Marshall was absolutely livid and wrote an angry attack on Hood in the North Sails newsletter. Commodore McCullough didn't say a word about it when we came in, but there was no doubt that he was unhappy. Yet there was also no doubt that mainsail selection was now up to Hood, since if McCullough insisted upon using the North sail, he would be on the spot if we lost the second race.

Business considerations must have played some part in Hood's decision to use his mainsail. It is a major mistake to think that the America's Cup is not big business. There is a lot of money and prestige tied up in the Cup and although sailmakers say that they lose money making 12-Meter sails, they more than make it all back in the long run if their sails are on a winning boat. But looking at the situation from the point of view of Ted Hood-the-skipper and not Ted Hood-the-sailmaker, I can see that he wanted to use gear in which he had the greatest trust. It wasn't enough that everybody else had confidence in the North main—he didn't, and he was the skipper. Perhaps he could never have total confidence in somebody else's product. For over twenty years, he had been winning races in all kinds of big boats with his own sails, and I'm sure that he was not happy with the prospect of losing this race or series because he had to worry about another sailmaker's sail. He was willing to take the risks of disobeying the syndicate manager, who was the Vice Commodore of the New York Yacht Club, of going against his crew's advice and, possibly, of losing the race.

I can understand Hood's decision because it showed how self-confident a good skipper has to be. To do well at winning sailboat races (as well as anything else), you have to have a strong, confident image of yourself as a winner. This means that you must have faith in your own judgment. Ted Hood obviously sees himself as a winner because he *is* a winner, and he clearly has faith in his own judgment. That's why he could and did take that risk. We did not win the America's Cup because we used the Hood mainsail instead of the North one. There were some other factors that were as, or more, important. One of them was having as skipper a man as able and as self-confident as Hood.

The start of the first race was pretty cut and dried. We circled the press boat a couple of times and then, with about three minutes to go, *Southern Cross* stalled just below the line, with her sails luffing on starboard tack and just a bit of headway. I chose to go to leeward of her, since the port end of the line was slightly favored, and we stalled there, too. With a little less than a minute to go, they backed her jib, tacked, and headed for the starboard end on port, and we trimmed our sails and headed for the port end. We crossed the line three seconds ahead, in about 10 knots of wind, and tacked to cover. Hood then took the wheel.

On the long port tack out to the layline—about nineteen minutes of sailing—it looked as though we were footing on them and they were pointing well, squeezing up under us. It was foggy, with about half a mile of visibility, so we could not see the mark. Halsey was keeping track of our position on a little computer, calling off the amount of time left to the layline. Meanwhile, we were both headed about 5 degrees and the distance between us had decreased about 150 yards. It looked to me as though they could cross us.

I told everybody that our strategy was to keep going until they tacked, and then to tack right under their bow in the safe leeward position so we would backwind them all the way to the mark. It meant that we had to tack perfectly. *Southern Cross* tacked, we sailed right up to them, and Ted tacked perfectly about a boat length to leeward. We never would have crossed them. The boats sailed equally for quite a while until, once again, we started to foot on them and they started to point on us.

Now it was important to know where the mark was. If we had overstood we were in great shape, if we were on the layline we were in good shape, but if we were not fetching, it was pretty bad. Halsey was unsure of the mark's position, but I eventually found it about 12 degrees off our lee bow— great news. We could have done several things then, one of which would be to simply head off for the mark. But we would not have gained much on *Southern Cross* if we had done that. What I decided to do was simply to foot a little more so we would squeeze out ahead of the Australians without tipping our hand. I told the crew to be just as quiet as possible as they eased the sheets and the traveler out very slowly.

After a while, they were five or six boat lengths to windward of us with the mark 20 degrees off our lee bow. I said, "Let's go for it, guys," Hood bore off for the mark and the crew set the spinnaker gear up. We rounded thirty-four seconds in the lead. (A movie of the race showed that *Southern Cross* hit this mark, but they did not reround it.) We gained throughout the rest of the race, although the final margin of four minutes, fifty-four seconds reflects the fact that the breeze died to about 5 knots. This race showed that *Southern Cross* was a fast boat upwind. Only poor navigation and tactics kept her from leading at the all-important first weather mark and perhaps going on to win the race.

At a press conference after the race, Alan Bond called me a "cowboy" who used "rodeo tactics" because I had yelled a few times at Jim Hardy about possible racing rule violations. I was only trying to keep Hardy on his toes and was not trying to take advantage of him. There is always a lot of talk between the crews in a good match-race start, anyway. When I was asked about Bond's comments in the press conference, I said that he seemed more upset about it than Hardy, and everybody laughed. I didn't want to give the impression that Bond's attack bothered me.

The second race's start was more exciting. It was held after a day's delay because of fog. It was blowing about 10 knots again and, not surprisingly, we were using the Hood mainsail—Ted having made his point. We tailed *Southern Cross* through the spectator fleet until, with about seven minutes to go, they tacked onto port right in front of us. We were converging at 8 1/2 knots, with Hood yelling, "Staabad, staabad!" in his New England accent. Hardy tried to tack to avoid us, but we had to alter course sharply only a few feet away. To give Hardy a good scare, I came as close as I could to them, and then I luffed up, yelled to put the protest flag up, and tacked. Our bow man, L.J. Edgecomb, came back aft with his eyes as big as saucers. He was sure we were going to cut them in half. We figured that there was no way we could lose the protest, so we stayed away from them at the start to keep out of trouble. We started together on starboard, with us to leeward, and Ted did a nice job of squeezing up under them and forcing them to tack after seven minutes. We covered, but they gained, tacked again, and crossed us, yet they did not cover and let us continue to the favored side of the course.

I don't like to sail away from my competition even when I'm behind, so I was getting pretty nervous about letting *Southern Cross* go off alone. What if the wind backed and favored them? I had no idea what Ted thought about the situation, since he didn't talk all that much, but I kept telling him what was happening and what I thought we should do. At the first tiny header, I told him we should tack back. We did, and a minute later we got a 5-degree lift, and then two more for a total lift of 15 degrees in about fifteen minutes. If they had covered when ahead, *Southern Cross* would have gained instead of us. Now we led at the weather mark by thirty-four seconds. The Aussies gained a little on the reaches, but we gradually opened up on the last legs of the twenty-four-mile Olympic course to win by one minute, eleven seconds. Once again, *Southern Cross* was a fast but poorly-sailed boat. If her crew had sailed at all intelligently, they might have been up two races on us.

Even though we won, we did not withdraw the protest. This was partly because they were counter-protesting, claiming that we bore off on them before the near-collision, and partly because we knew we were right. I represented *Courageous* in the protest hearing and, oddly enough, *Southern Cross* was represented not by Hardy or another crew member but by a lawyer. There had been a lot of hard feelings during and after the 1970 America's Cup, when *Gretel II* was disqualified (correctly, I think) from a race she had won for hitting and fouling *Intrepid* at a start. The Australians claimed that the New York Yacht Club would do anything to keep the Cup, even to the point of changing the rules. In 1974, there was an international jury to hear protests. It was chaired by Beppe Croce, the president of the International Yacht Racing Union. Bond still didn't like the arrangement, so he hired a lawyer to study the racing rules and represent him in any hearings.

The foul at the start of the second America's Cup race. *Southern Cross*, on port, tried to cross *Courageous*. When Jim Hardy saw that he could not make it, he tacked, but Dennis Conner still had to alter course. *(Photos by Bill Robinson.)*

In any case, both protests were thrown out. I think the jury disallowed our protest because we had won the race and because there had been no contact. It was the first time in my sailing experience that somebody was not disqualified for tacking too close to another boat when he was not able to find any witnesses on his defense. In fact, just after the near-collision, I yelled to a nearby powerboat, "Will you be witnesses for me?" I didn't know that on board were the members of the jury, with a full, close-up view of the entire incident.

Bond became very upset, publicly blaming his crew as well as the New York Yacht Club for his boat's record. The yacht club was at fault, he said, because it had not allowed *Southern Cross* to practice on the Cup course and the boat's crew had not learned about such wind shifts as the lift that gave us the lead in the second race. That was nonsense, because they were the ones who found that shift first. Bond then made the fatal mistake of changing a fast boat, putting on an experimental rudder, using different sails, and replacing both the navigator and the tactician.

After three days of delay due to fog, calm, and a lay day, we started the third race on September 16, in a puffy, moderate northwest breeze. We were both early at the start. *Courageous* was the leeward boat, so we jibed onto port, tacked, recrossed the line, and started at the favored end. It took Hardy longer to react to the recall, and we had a good lead—forty-five seconds at the first mark and five minutes, twenty-seven seconds at the finish. *Southern Cross* was not going as well as she had in the first two races. The fourth race, on the seventeenth, was a walk

Courageous (left) and *Southern Cross* stalling before the start of the fourth America's Cup race. The Australians tried to stop their boat and get away from Conner by backing their mainsail, but the Americans stayed in control by using the same trick. *(Photo by Stanley Rosenfeld.)*

away. *Southern Cross* lost all her way while we stalled before the start and we had a good twenty-second lead at the gun. Our margin at the first mark was one minute, nineteen seconds, and we gained over two minutes on each of the next two windward legs to win in moderate air by seven minutes, nineteen seconds.

Why did we win by so much? The boats were equally fast upwind. The first legs of the first two races show that much. Their tactics were not good—the first two races show that, too. But I think our real advantage was in attention to detail. *Courageous* had been racing hard since June, and most of the bugs had been eliminated. Except for the controversy over the mainsail, I think we had a pretty good idea of what made the boat go fast, even though Hood and I were relatively new to the boat. If we had been in Bond's shoes after the first two races, I don't think that we would have made the drastic changes in equipment and personnel that he did because we would have known that our boat was going well. It wasn't gear or sails or hulls that made the difference. People and such intangibles as self-confidence, hard work, good organization, and a winning attitude did it, just as they always do in racing.

Once the celebrating was over, when I left Newport I felt like a hired hand going home in the afternoon. It was great helping to defend the America's Cup, but it would have been even better to have been part of a winning team for the entire summer. The 1974 America's Cup summer taught me a lot about boats and even more about how people act under pressure. I sailed in three 12-Meters—*Mariner, Valiant,* and *Courageous*—which were the worst and the best boats racing at Newport in 1974, and the differences between them were striking. For instance, *Courageous* steered much better than *Mariner.* They were as dissimilar as a Cadillac on a highway and a dune buggy in the sand. But they were also similar in some ways. Twelves are such heavy, finely shaped boats that they go fast all the time and can also point very well. They are relatively easy boats to steer, but take quite a while to learn how to steer well. For example, you can steer with the genoa luff tell tales both streaming aft perfectly, as you do in other boats, and not be right, since you go faster and faster as you bear off until, as on an ice boat, the tell tales may still be streaming but you may be close-hauled in a true wind that is actually a beam reach. Sometimes you actually have to slow up and wait for the apparent wind to go aft so you can point the boat.

Because the boats are so sensitive, big, and expensive, the pressures on the sailors and syndicate managers are enormous. It is a rule that the skippers be members of the New York Yacht Club, and it is expected that all involved are socially presentable. One of the reasons why it took so long for Ted Turner to be asked to sail a Twelve was that he did not quite fit into the Eastern Establishment's image of itself. This is why it is so hard to be selected as helmsman of a Twelve. Judging by the changes in the afterguards in three of the four boats in 1974 and of two of the three boats in 1977, I should add "and to remain helmsman."

The pressure can be so intense that it can strain personal relationships. This is one of the best reasons why friendship and serious sailing should not mix. Bob McCullough and Bob Bavier were good friends before the America's Cup, but it must have been hard on both of them when McCullough replaced Bavier with Hood at the eleventh hour. Bavier, to his credit, didn't pout. He simply said, "I think I'm the man for the job, but if I'm not, I'm going to stick around and do everything I can to help. You can count on me." I really admired that. It must have been equally difficult for McCullough. He knew he was doing the right thing, so he couldn't say, "I'm sorry," but he must have felt embarrassed and emotional. I know that I felt uncomfortable around Bavier because I was one of the people who replaced him.

And how did McCullough feel placing this million-dollar boat for which he was responsible into new hands just a few days before the Cup series was to start? When I say "hands," I also mean "eyes." With the deck-sweeping booms on those boats, the helmsman, steering from the windward side, could not see anything to leeward, so as tactician I was partly responsible for making sure this sixty-thousand-pound boat sailing at 9 knots wouldn't run into something.

Simply having to win a trophy that has never been lost is a heavy responsibility, too. In 1974, with all sorts of rumors going about that *Southern Cross* was a super-boat, it seemed that it might finally be the year for the Cup to leave the New York Yacht Club's trophy room. The pressure of this responsibility may be the reason why so many skippers lost their jobs that summer, why McCullough was so insistent about Hood using the North mainsail, and why Hood was so obstinate about using his own sail. Suddenly, America's Cup sailing had, like the SORC and the Olympics, ceased being a pastime and started being serious business. I enjoyed the pressure and responsibility that summer, and I think I did pretty well under it. I did not, however, enjoy seeing what it did to other people. Most of us want to leave pressure behind at the office, but if you want to win in sailing today you had better be prepared to face tension on the race course, too.

III

Ocean Racing

CHAPTER 6

Preparing a
Winning Boat

THERE WAS a different sort of sailing challenge to look
forward to when I arrived back home in San Diego after the
Cup—the 1975 SORC. The Southern Ocean Racing Conference is the most important distance-racing series in North
America, and one of the most important in the world. I sailed
in my first SORC in 1968, in Marty Gleich's Redline 41, *Hallelujah*. The crew included Lowell North and Dick Deaver,
but we were so inexperienced at ocean racing that a couple
of us didn't even bring foul weather gear. We finished second
in our class and Marty improved so much that he sold the boat
rather than go back to San Diego and dominate everybody.
For me, the most important event in ocean racing had been
the Rumsey Series for the championship of San Diego, but
that SORC opened my eyes. There were so many good looking boats at the "Circuit" (as it's called) that *Hallelujah* just got
lost at the docks. It was obvious that we had been living in a
vacuum in Southern California.

I continued going south every February, sailing the five or

six races off Florida and Nassau in other people's boats, until I began to think how nice it would be to sail my own boat in a Circuit. In 1974, I had a Ranger 32, *Carpetbagger*, there and with Lowell, O.J. Young, Peter Barrett, and some other good people crewing for me, we did not do all that well. Sailing in a fleet of One Tonners, we discovered that if you wanted to win, you had to have a custom-built boat. Some of the best One Tonners (boats about thirty-five feet long and rating 27.5 under the International Offshore Rule) at that SORC had been designed by Doug Peterson and built by Carl Eichenlaub in San Diego. Doug had been brought up in San Diego, where he and my wife, Judy, went to the same school and where, as a teenager, he worked for a local yacht designer named Skip Calkins. I and my sailing friends at San Diego Yacht Club didn't know him very well, and he eventually disappeared into the Navy in Japan. Finally, in early 1973, Doug appeared again in San Diego with some drawings of a boat, and he asked everybody he knew what they thought of it. I don't think I was alone in telling him that it didn't look very fast. It was a thirty-four-foot One Tonner, and compared with the hottest boat around at the time, the thirty-seven-foot Ranger One Tonner that Gary Mull had designed, it looked awfully small. Doug eventually worked a deal out with Carl Eichenlaub, and Carl built the boat out of wood in his yard on Shelter Island, with Doug begging or borrowing paint and gear to finish her off within the approximately fifteen thousand dollar budget he had available. He asked Lowell North for a good deal on the sails, but Lowell didn't want to have anything to do with the boat.

Doug asked me to sail *Ganbare* (which, he said, means the kind of good luck that a kamakazi pilot has) in the 1973 One Ton North American Championship in May at San Diego. But I said no. The boat was ridiculously small, I thought, and, with only one winch in the cockpit, she looked really underrigged and unseaworthy. So Doug sailed the boat himself. After a couple of days I called the yacht club for the standings and to my disbelief they told me that *Ganbare* was winning. "You're kidding," I said. "It must be really shifty out there." But it wasn't shifty. *Ganbare* just powered away from everybody at the start and won the series easily. Later, Doug offered to sell me the boat for twenty thousand dollars, but I turned him down, so he and Lowell (who now was a believer) took her to the 1973 One Ton Worlds in Sardinia, which they would have won if they hadn't been penalized for missing a buoy. We're so used to seeing Peterson designs winning ocean races that we forget that only a few years ago he was a struggling young designer who had trouble getting his first boat launched.

With the success of *Ganbare* and others of Doug's One Tonners and the growth of popularity in level racing, where boats of a given rating sail against each other without handicap, I figured that a Peterson One Tonner would be a good boat for the 1975 SORC. The chances were good that we would do well, so I didn't feel that I was risking my money on a boat with bad resale value.

Organizing a new custom boat for a series like the SORC takes a lot of planning and attention to details. I've done it now with *Stinger* for the 1975 SORC, and with *High Roler* and *Williwaw* for the 1977 and 1978 Circuits, and there's no doubt in my mind that the priorities are in this order:

> FIRST, make sure you have the best-designed and best-built boat available. Even the very best crews can't win these days with a boat that's off the pace.
>
> SECOND, get the best possible navigator, helmsmen, and other crew members.
>
> THIRD, get the best sails.

I started organizing for the boat that eventually became *Stinger* even before I went east for the 1974 America's Cup. I had sold my interest in a carpet business and was thinking about going into partnership in boat-building with Carl Eichenlaub and Jack Mueller, an Ohio Lightning sailor who

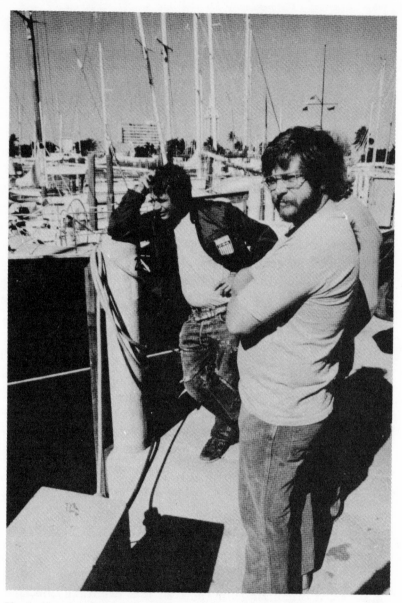

Yacht designer Doug Peterson (foreground) and Conner's Lightning skipper and boat-builder Carl Eichenlaub (rear) at the 1977 SORC. *(Photo by John Rousmaniere.)*

then owned Eichenlaub's yard. I talked those two into joining me in a One Tonner for the 1975 Circuit, and they built *Kingfish*, a Peterson sistership to *Ganbare*, while I was at Newport. Then Nick Frazee, a San Diego businessman, bought Mueller out and Jack took *Kingfish* in partial payment. So Frazee and Eichenlaub owed me a One Tonner.

I couldn't have been luckier, because in the meantime Doug developed a One Tonner that was a little faster than *Ganbare*, especially in heavy air and when reaching. This new design, which won the 1974 One Ton Worlds, was a little longer and beamier than *Ganbare* and rated the same as the earlier boat. Since the SORC is usually sailed in good winds with a lot of reaching, I wanted this design, but I asked Doug to improve the light-air performance a little by giving her a slightly taller rig.

Doug and Carl recommended that we build the boat out of aluminum, which Carl was unfamiliar with but which they said produced a stiff boat that was light in the ends and cheaper than a wooden boat. Racing-boat hulls have to be stiff and strong so that they don't "oilcan," or deflect, under the stresses of the rigging and the waves. They have to be as light as possible in the bow and stern so that they don't pitch too much in seas, and so waste a lot of energy going up and down when they should be putting all that energy into going forward. They should also be relatively inexpensive because the owner wants to minimize his risk. Unless you are extremely wealthy, you can't afford to lose borrowed money on a boat.

Carl understands all of this, and he also knows that the hull and the keel have to be built exactly the way that the designer drew them. Carl can build a boat very quickly. *Stinger* took only twenty-two working days. He started about mid-October, 1974, and we were sailing at Thanksgiving.

One aspect of design that I have learned to pay a lot of attention to is the interior. The day it was time to put the bunks in, Carl called me up and inquired what I wanted. I asked him what Doug's plans had called for. He said, "Are you kidding? There are no plans for the interior. You'd better get down here." I hadn't even thought about an interior but I went down, looked it over, and told them how I wanted it. There were no frills, like a table or an enclosed head, and I borrowed a lot of ideas from Gary Mull's Ranger One Tonner. My main concern was with arranging the bunks so that she could sleep the off-watch of four men all on the windward side to help the righting moment. On each side she had a quarter berth with a pipe berth above, plus settee and pilot berths in the main cabin. I later did the same thing with *High Roler* (a Peterson forty-six-footer I sailed in the 1977 SORC), only we had to sleep five on one side.

There is very little forward of the mast, where weight can really increase the pitching moment. So you start in the center of the boat and work aft. This doesn't necessarily mean that you strip the boat out, with no woodwork. If you own a boat, you want her to be attractive enough below so you can take your friends below for a drink, and you want to make her comfortable for long-distance races. A lot of people, like Lowell North, strip a boat out entirely, but I like a little wood, an ice box, and a small oven for heating up meals. An oven may add twenty or thirty pounds to the boat's weight, but in the center of the boat it doesn't hurt performance and it helps the resale value. In all, the stove, cushions, extra bulkheads, ceiling, and other amenities in *High Roler* increased her interior weight by only two hundred pounds.

Another important item is a good, reasonably comfortable navigator's station, preferably in a place where the navigator can talk directly to the helmsman. In Florida and the Bahamas, where navigation is very tricky, good communication between the navigator and the skipper is crucial. In both *Stinger* and *High Roler*, the navigator worked under the bridge deck and could talk directly to the helmsman through a cockpit port.

On deck, there are no worries about balancing efficiency and pride of ownership, although once again you have got to

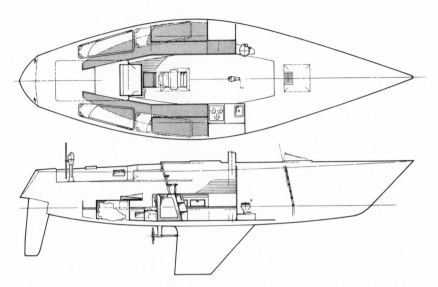

High Roler's plans show a clean, flush deck and a simple, open interior. The most important consideration when planning an ocean racer's interior is to allow the entire off-watch (five men in this boat) to sleep to windward. *(Drawing by Bill Hardin.)*

reconsider resale value. For example, I might have used a tiller instead of a wheel in *High Roler* except that very few people interested in buying her would like a tiller-steered forty-six-footer. Tillers are more sensitive, and it's easier to see the genoa and the waves using a tiller and hiking stick, but a wheel is much more popular. Of course, there was no question about using a tiller in *Stinger,* which was a small boat.

Otherwise on deck, you try to centralize the winches as much as possible so the boat can be sailed with a minimum of effort by a few men. Originally I planned to sail *High Roler* with only nine men—we carried eight in *Stinger.* Except during sail changes and tacks and jibes, it takes only two or three guys to sail a boat. One is the helmsman, another is the sheet trimmer for the genoa or spinnaker, and the third is a winch grinder and spare man. I thought that if we just had those three men on deck, we wouldn't need another two guys in a watch up there freezing and not getting any rest. So I planned to assign three to a watch plus two rovers. These would be two strong, good men who would be sleeping in foul weather gear and on call for winch-grinding and mast work during maneuvers. The ninth man would be the navigator. Of course the deck would have to be carefully laid out for such a short crew. As it was, I eventually decided to carry eleven men, with five on a watch. Deciding who those eight or nine or eleven men are is the second most important decision after the one about the hull. I like the luxury of having many good guys on board, but if you have too many people, you carry excess weight. In a long race, you carry about 150 pounds of food and gear for each man on board.

The navigator is very important not only because he tells you where you are but because, if he's good, he can tell you about weather patterns and current. This is especially important in the SORC, because weather fronts come through quickly and because of the Gulf Stream, which, because it runs as fast as four knots, can make all the difference in a race. One of the very best navigators was Ben Mitchell, from Los Angeles, and he agreed to come along in *Stinger*.

I wanted a total of four helmsmen—three besides myself —and I asked Lowell North, Gary Wiseman (a young employee of Lowell's who steers very well), and Jon Andron (who has won Transpac Races to Honolulu) to come and steer. Basic talent had a lot to do with this selection, and so did attitude. Jon Andron, for instance, has a strong, positive winning attitude that is really good for crew morale.

Myself, Ben, Lowell, Gary, and Jon, plus a "guest expert" in some races—those were the members of our nucleus. I then needed two guys to run the foredeck. Anybody on the boat could have done this reasonably well, although on larger boats such as *High Roler* the crew jobs have to be more specialized, but it was still important to get two good men. I asked Bob Burns and Dave Miller. Miller was in charge of boat maintenance during the SORC.

Finally, the sails. All but one of *Stinger*'s sails were made by Lowell's loft. The exception was a Hood reaching spinnaker called a flanker, which is cut differently from the North starcut and which I liked when I saw it in use on the 12-Meters. Of course Lowell disagreed, but I thought it was especially effective in light-air close-reaching. We also carried an old spinnaker that I had kept from *Carpetbagger*, my 1974 SORC boat. It was too small for a One Tonner, but, because of its size, it was an excellent chute for reaching in heavy air and helped us do very well in the Miami-Nassau Race.

After *Stinger* was launched, the first thing we did was to get her to rate as low as possible. By making adjustments here and there, we were able to give her a sail area slightly larger than the one we had thought would get her to rate at the intended 27.5 feet. We got the crew together for practice. Ben came down from Los Angeles every weekend to work with the compass and the electronics. We had a chance to look at the sails and have them recut at the loft, and we took every opportunity we could to sail in heavy air.

To our surprise, we discovered that the boat would lose control and broach in conditions that really shouldn't have bothered us—on a beam reach as little as 20 knots of wind. We began to get that uncomfortable feeling that we weren't in control of our own destiny downwind, so, against Doug's and everybody else's advice, I increased the size of the rudder. This gave us a little more wetted surface in light air, but I like having the security blanket of being able to steer all the time. That large rudder and the small Ranger 32 spinnaker made us very potent when reaching in heavy air.

I was also pretty conservative in my selection of a mast. I had broken a mast the year before in *Carpetbagger*, and I agreed with Ted Turner's dictum of, "Put the spinnaker up and let God take it down," with no fear for the rig. Add to this my relative lack of experience in heavy winds—I always feel like going inside when the wind blows hard—and you see I really had a dread of masts breaking. So I asked for a large section but, because of a mistake, ended up with a telephone pole that belonged on a Two Tonner and that really embarrassed Lowell, who likes to have very small, clean spars. Yet I was content when we went out in the surf, sometimes with the whole boat leaping out of the water, and the mast stayed in. At least we didn't need running backstays to keep it straight.

We marked all our leads and halyard positions for various sails at various wind strengths, raced a little off San Diego, packed up *Stinger*, and trucked her to New Orleans. Racing against a few much bigger boats, such as an Ericson 39 and a Newport 41, showed that we were fast, so we were encouraged when we picked her up in New Orleans for our sail to St. Petersburg. Ben Mitchell came along, and he was great. He's a lot more than just a navigator, because he's always attentive to details such as how much water we have aboard and how many matches we have so we can light the stove.

At one stage on the sail south I was on deck and saw some waterspouts; I yelled below to ask Ben if they were dangerous. "Waterspouts?", he said. "Don't worry about them."

I said, "They look pretty close, Ben. Don't you want to take a look?"

So he stuck his head up and as soon as he saw them he yelled, "Jesus, let's get the hell out of here!" Luckily they missed us.

Before the SORC that year there was a match race series just for One Tonners—a perfect opportunity to learn something more about our boat. There we found that our number three genoa was too big for heavy air, so we ordered a number four (that we never did use), and we discovered that we didn't have a lot of speed in light air, at least against Ted Hood in his centerboard One Tonner, which beat us in the series.

During the next few days, we tuned against a boat named *Moody Blue* that her designer, Mark Soverel, was sailing. She rated a foot-and-a-half higher than we did, but we were able to keep up. We worked especially hard on our light-air upwind speed. With the help of Dick Deaver, who ran a North Sails loft in Seal Beach, California, and who would be sailing against us in the Circuit in another One Tonner, we learned how to use our double-head rig in light air. In this arrangement you set two jibs, a lightweight jib topsail and, under it, a genoa staysail. The total area is greater than that of the light number one genoa alone and the aerodynamic flow is better. A boat usually can't point quite as high with the double-head rig as she can with a genoa, but will go a lot faster and is therefore usually a better rig unless the water is perfectly smooth and speed isn't a problem. The problem with the double-head rig is that it is hard to tack and, because there are three sails up instead of two, it is more difficult to trim properly. Tuning against *Moody Blue*, we developed so much confidence in the double-head rig that we decided to leave the light number one genoa ashore. We would use the jib top and staysail upwind in light air—up to about 12 or 14 knots apparent wind (about 7 or 8 knots true wind)—and the heavy number one genoa when it was windier, until we had to shorten down to the number two.

During the match race series we looked carefully at the other boats' jib leads and compared them with our own. Since we were so new to our boat, we figured that the more experienced sailors with the older boats—especially Ted Hood —probably knew better than we did where to trim their jibs. I went aboard the other boats when nobody was around and took some measurements off the marks on the tracks or decks and compared the angles with the ones on *Stinger*. First, I measured the distance from the stem to the lead position and then the distance between the starboard and port lead positions. With those two dimensions, it was easy to measure the angle, using the formula for a circle's circumference, 2π R. Here, R was the distance in inches from the stem to the lead position. Multiply that by 6.28 (2π) and you have the circumference of the circle whose center is at the stem. Divide that by 360 and you have the number of inches for each degree of angle. On a One Tonner, that was 5 1/4 inches per degree. Take half of the distance in inches between the lead positions on the port and starboard sides and divide that by 5 1/4 and you have the angle to the lead in degrees. I learned this technique in Stars, where everybody knew that the 7 1/2-degree line was 11 1/4 inches from the centerline.

What these comparisons told us was that the track for our number two genoa was well inboard of everybody else's. This was because our track was lined up on deck pointed right toward the stem, so the smaller genoas, with the leads farther forward, had the same lead angle as the number one. This is wrong, since, as it gets windier, you want to move the leads slightly outboard in order to decrease heeling moment. The other boats' tracks were more or less parallel to the centerline, so that leads farther forward were a degree or two more outboard than those farther aft. We also found out that the leads for the number three were too far outboard, which meant that we couldn't point the way we should have.

The solution was to put down two short, eighteen-inch lengths of track on each side of the boat, one track for the number two genoa and one track for the number three. One of my rules in sailboat racing is to have the same basic equipment as everybody else. I wanted to know that if all the One Tonners changed down to number three genoas at the same time, we would have the same lead position as everybody else. That way, nobody could beat us on equipment alone.

Going into the SORC's first race, a 103-miler to Anclote Key that started and finished at St. Petersburg, I felt pretty good. We had a good design and a good boat. We had one of the best, if not the best, crews. And we had a fine sail inventory. I knew that our primary competition would come from Dick Deaver, sailing a Ron Holland-designed One Tonner named *Bootlegger*. Since we both rated the same, all we had to do was beat him around the course to win our class; but to win the entire Circuit, we had to do consistently well on handicap against boats as large as Jim Kilroy's new seventy-nine-foot ketch, *Kialoa III*. We had to hope it would be a good series for smaller boats.

CHAPTER 7

The 1975 SORC

THE SORC consists of six races. In 1975, the first race, on January 31, was the 103-mile Anclote Key Race off St. Petersburg. Then, on February 5, came a race from St. Petersburg down around the Florida keys and back up to Ft. Lauderdale, just north of Miami. At 403 miles this was the longest of the six races and counted the most in the point scores. The 132-mile Ocean Triangle was next, on February 14, going from Miami across the Gulf Stream to Great Isaac lighthouse, in the Bahamas, then back across to Ft. Lauderdale and south again to the finish at Miami. The fourth race, on February 22, was the 38-mile Lipton Cup day race off Miami. Next came the Miami-Nassau Race, which started on February 24 and ran 190 miles—the second most important race in the Circuit. And the sixth and last race, the 35-mile Nassau Cup, was held on February 28 off Nassau.

The Circuit is arranged so you can sail the whole series and still take only eight or ten days off from work. That winter I flew back and forth from California to Florida six times in order to race, run my business, and see something of my wife and daughters. The hassle is worth it, since the best ocean racing boats and sailors in America, and some of the best in the world, are there for the series. The winds are usually good—usually a little stronger than they are in most other sailing areas—and, once the fleet gets around to the Gulf Stream on the east side of Florida, the weather is pleasant, although it can be cold even that far south in January and February. The Admiral's Cup series, held every second summer in England, is often called the ocean racing world championship, but I think the racing in the SORC is better run and often just as good.

The Anclote Key Race started with a light-air close reach, in which we used the Hood flanker spinnaker to get a one-minute lead after the first few miles. The wind came ahead and, as we beat out Tampa Bay, we sailed up through the larger boats that had started ahead of us. We tacked around the buoy at the entrance of the bay and sailed inshore, preferring to be there on the beat north to Anclote Key because it looked fluky outside. When we got to the turning mark in what we thought was great shape, with a good lead over the rest of our class, we saw another boat just inside us. It was *Bootlegger*, and we rounded the mark together, set spinnakers, and started to match race down the shore to the finish. We hit a wind line first and got away from them and into what seemed a good lead, but two other boats got by us by staying farther out in the Gulf of Mexico, so we finished third in our class and fourteenth overall. It was disappointing, particularly since we had done so well in the first half of the race, but at least we beat Dick Deaver in *Bootlegger*.

Bootlegger led us by a good half mile going out of Tampa Bay after the start of the Lauderdale Race, partly because we were over early at the start and lost some time returning for our restart. We reached for a while on the leg down to Rebecca Shoals, the rock at the keys that is a turning mark, and then the wind backed and we had a beat into a shifty wind, tacking on headers. When the sun came up the next morning, all we could see were big boats—and a lot of them. The other One Tonners were all behind us. The wind began to go back into the west, so we tacked short of the starboard tack layline and were lifted right up to Rebecca, which we rounded in the evening.

The wind veered some more and increased after we set the three-quarter-ounce spinnaker. I was sleeping but woke right up when we had a few blasts of wind and the boat took off. I jumped up, looked into the cockpit, and suggested to Lowell, Gary, and O.J. Young, who were on watch, that they change to a heavier spinnaker.

Lowell said, "It really isn't blowing very hard, and this sail is new and pretty strong."

"Well, how fast are we going?" I asked.

"Ten knots."

"Ten knots! What do you *mean* it's not blowing very hard!"

Then O.J., who is from New Orleans and sails in the Gulf a lot, said, "Oh, go back to sleep. It always blows harder in the beginning of these fronts than it does later on."

So I went below. I was no sooner back in my bunk than I heard a huge BANG as the spinnaker exploded. Lowell later said that the puffs went right up to 35 as soon as I went below. They put the one-and-a-half-ounce spinnaker up and I made Lowell help me sew up that light chute. But we hadn't lost anything and were still up with some really big boats. After the race we learned that *Charisma*, a fifty-four-footer, was then only an hour ahead of us.

When the sun came up on the third day, we were running in very light air, still ahead of the other One Tonners. It was happy to have the light spinnaker back in one piece, but we looked astern and saw some spinnakers getting closer. We recognized *Bootlegger*'s chute, and one on another Peterson One Tonner, *Country Woman*, sailed by a sailmaker named

Bob Barton. We got a little more breeze and headed up toward shore, where those two seemed to be doing well, even though Ben Mitchell kept warning me that we were getting out of the Gulf Stream (which flows rapidly toward Ft. Lauderdale). But there was no way that I'd let those guys get by inside of us in more wind.

Soon we were only a couple of hundred yards apart—we had lost that huge lead—and we were close-reaching on port tack in a building wind. These were *Stinger*'s conditions, but *Country Woman*, which had more or less the same hull, also did well on that point of sail. For mile after mile, the three of us sailed like one-designs. We slowly opened up a three-boat-length lead on Barton and a ten-boat-length lead on Deaver. After a while we were perhaps a mile up on Deaver, and at Alligator Reef—where we all should have begun to harden up to parallel the Florida coast—Deaver started to sag off to leeward. We couldn't understand it, but pretty soon he began to gain on us. Ben eventually figured out that he was out in favorable current in the Gulf Stream while we were inside in no current at all. Dick had figured this out two hours earlier than we had, and had that much advantage. Since we had to cover *Bootlegger* for the series (Barton had a bad first race), we bore off to get into the current, too. But Deaver headed off some more and kept gaining. We ended up bearing off almost 25 degrees and gained on *Country Woman*, but Deaver caught us—gaining a mile in only four hours.

We sailed boat against boat, hard on the wind in a northerly, with the whole crew sitting on the weather rail all night. When the wind got shifty, we started tacking on headers as large as 20 degrees and caught *Bootlegger*. We finished only five hours behind the seventy-nine-foot *Kialoa*, and there were only sixteen boats ahead of us, so we and the other One Tonners dominated the standings. The next One Tonner to finish was *Country Woman*, twenty minutes back; Deaver in *Bootlegger* dropped back to fourth after going too far inshore near the finish. So we now had a first and a third in class and a first and and a fourteenth overall, and we were leading the Southern Circuit.

The third race of the 1975 SORC was a 132-miler called the Ocean Triangle, and though we did not win, we did well enough to keep our series lead. The race started off Miami and the first leg was east across the Gulf Stream to Stirrup Key, in the Bahamas. The wind was light and behind us, and we were afraid that the strong current in the Stream would sweep us far to the north if we sailed the rhumb line course. So we jibed to starboard right after the start to make some ground to the south in the slack water and back eddies near the Florida shore. We hoped to go far enough to give us a good sailing angle on a broad reach across the Stream—you always want to be going as fast as you can when you cross currents —but the wind did not cooperate. It increased in velocity and veered from the northwest to the northeast, so we had to beat across to Stirrup, and we were way back, the most leeward boat in our class. (The next year, I did this in *Charisma* and it paid off.)

We were back with the smaller Class E boats, but it became very shifty toward the end of the leg and we started to gain. Finally, we crossed just behind a boat that looked like *Country Woman,* and, three tacks later, we were well ahead of them. We then had a spinnaker reach back across the Stream to Palm Beach, followed by a close reach to the finish at Miami. When the sun came up, we saw *Bootlegger* ahead of us, and she beat us in by two-and-one-half minutes. This gave us a second in class and fourteenth overall, and we were still leading.

The next race, The Lipton Cup, was only thirty-eight miles, but it was the one that broke *Bootlegger* and gave us the series. It was a broad reach north from Miami to Ft. Lauderdale and a beat to return. *Stinger* and *Bootlegger* sailed all the way to Ft. Lauderdale within two boat lengths of each other, and we rounded just ahead of them. Instead of sailing close-hauled toward the finish, Deaver bore off to head toward shore, away from the head current in the Stream. Of course, we reached off to cover them. In the meantime, all the other One Tonners, which were sailing a more direct, shorter course, were gaining on us.

Eventually, Deaver headed up to close-hauled, and we did the same, and then he tacked and we covered. We sailed back toward the other boats, and the two of us tacked just ahead of them. We were just able to pinch up under *Bootlegger* and give her a lot of backwind. A Ranger 37 sneaked between the two of us, and we won the class and took fourth overall, with *Bootlegger* third in class and eighth overall.

We needed a good finish in the Miami-Nassau Race, the second longest in the Circuit, to protect our big lead. We started in a tight reach with our little Ranger 32 spinnaker up and pulled away from everybody except *Country Woman*, which cut inside us at Stirrup Key because Ben Mitchell was conservative about cutting it too fine. Why risk the series by running aground? *Country Woman* just beat us to Nassau, and we were 1–2 in class and fleet. With a first and a second in the two most important races in the Circuit, we now had a big lead over *Inflation*, another Peterson One Tonner sailed by a bunch of Hawaiians that had come on strong in the late races. All we had to do in the last race, a day race off Nassau, was not foul out. We finished first in class again and third overall (mainly because the course was too short for the time allowance—I protested the race but the race committee threw the protest out), and *Stinger* had won the SORC by 29.25 points. Seven out of the top ten boats were One Tonners. *Inflation*, *Bootlegger*, and *Country Woman* were second, third, and fourth overall.

I had hoped to sell *Stinger* after the Circuit to somebody who might want to use her in the One Ton Worlds at Newport, Rhode Island, that fall. Three or four people had expressed an interest in her, but when we came into the dock after the Nassau Cup, there was Ted Turner, standing with

Jesse Philips, owner of the fifty-four-footer, *Charisma*. Turner had won Class B in his forty-eight-footer, *Tenacious*, (including winning two races overall) and *Charisma* had been third in Class B. I hadn't seen Turner much since the *Mariner* days the summer before, but he came right up and congratulated me and said, "I'm going to buy your boat!"

"Good deal," I said.

"How much do you want for her?", he asked. I said the price was sixty thousand dollars.

"You have a deal," Turner said. "And now that you don't have a boat any more, I've got a new boat for you to sail."

He took me over to Jesse Philips and introduced us, although, of course, we had met. Jesse was full of enthusiasm about our win. "Congratulations, fantastic! I've been rooting for you all along. By the way, why don't you come sail my boat for me now that you don't have one any more?"

There I was getting ready to get out of it, and I was right back in it again. I sold *Stinger* to Turner, using a cocktail napkin as a bill of sale, took my personal gear off her, and went over to have a look at *Charisma*.

Jesse had seemed like a nice guy. He was the head of Philips Industries, in Dayton, Ohio, and had only recently become interested in sailing. Everybody said that he would do anything to help make *Charisma* win. This was his third *Charisma*. The first had been a stock fiberglass boat that had done well on the Great Lakes. The second was a custom Sparkman & Stephens design that had done very well in international competition in the early seventies; this one was a fifty-four-footer, also designed by Sparkman & Stephens and built of aluminum. This was her first season, and a lot of people were disappointed that she hadn't done better in the SORC. Some thought she could have been sailed better.

The Admiral's Cup was coming up that summer and the selection committee had not yet met. This is an ocean racing series held off England in August of odd-numbered years. Three boats from each country sail in it, and the cup goes to

Stinger reaching in the final race of the 1975 SORC. Dennis Conner, playing the spinnaker sheet with a drink in his hand, shows how relaxed he was, knowing that he had already clinched the first-place trophy. *(Photo by Bahamas News Bureau.)*

the country with the best team score. Because so many very good sailors and boats go to it, the Admiral's Cup is considered the ocean racing championship of the world. Of course, Jesse wanted very much to go, but it looked as though he would have trouble getting selected. Turner had an excellent chance, as did Ted Hood, who had done well in the SORC in a forty-foot Two Tonner, but the third slot on the United States team was up for grabs. *Stinger* was too small to qualify. I had my doubts, if only because *Charisma* had been kicked around so easily by *Tenacious* and I didn't feel like playing second fiddle to Turner again. But I knew that sailing Jesse's boat would be like sailing my own boat, only all the money and support that I would have been unable to find would be there. She was the best boat Olin Stephens could design; she had the best sails North Sails could build; she had the nicest owner you could find. Sailing *Charisma* would be like dying and going to heaven. When she was selected for the team, I looked forward to a great summer, sailing both with and against my two skippers of the summer before, Ted Turner and Ted Hood.

CHAPTER 8

The Admiral's Cup

TAKING OVER the skipper's job in a boat is never easy, but when she is a boat as big as *Charisma* for a series as important as the Admiral's Cup, it means a lot of careful preparation. My first visit to her told me that she was a beautiful flat-out racing boat, with an excellent mast, an efficient deck layout, and a good, though stripped-out, interior. I went over her with some care and studied the plans and polar diagrams that Olin Stephens sent to me. I talked over with Jesse some possible modifications that might improve her rating, and then, in May, I began commuting to New York on weekends for tune-up sailing and races on Long Island Sound before she was to be sailed to England. As I had the summer before, I became very familiar with the art of finding cheap transcontinental flights by staggering east- and west-bound halves of special tickets. Making twelve trips for a total of about two thousand dollars sounds expensive, but it was a lot less expensive than having my own boat, even a Star. It was the cheapest summer I'd had in a long time.

In the east, the first thing we did was to take a really careful look at all the sails. We then marked the correct halyard tensions and lead positions for all conditions and evaluated the polar diagrams with instruments and a computer. On these big boats, you've got to know how fast you can go, expecially sailing off the wind, when tacking downwind can make a lot of difference.

We raced several overnight races on Long Island Sound, which was a lot different from the sailing I'd done in Florida and California. In those areas, boat speed is more important than local knowledge, but on the Sound, playing the shores and the tides can make all the difference between winning and doing poorly. It would be hard to learn to become a world-class sailor on Long Island Sound. Young sailors there don't learn enough about making a boat go fast because they spend so much time worrying about current and wind shifts. World and Olympic championships are almost always held in fair wind and tide, where boat speed really matters.

All this time, I was working closely with the crew to find the best people for each job. Unlike a small boat, *Charisma*, which had thirteen in crew, requires specialization. The loads are so much larger and the gear is so much more complicated that you have to select crew members for their skills at special jobs. Of course we had a navigator—two in fact, Halsey Herreshoff and Peter Lawson, and each stood a watch as a helmsman. We had a sail-trimmer for each watch, Jon Wright and Steve Prime, who were in charge of trimming the genoa and spinnaker. Each watch had a bow man—L.J. Edgecomb and Steve Liracas—whose job was to keep the halyards straight and to hook up new sails for changes. Then there were winch grinders and mast men, who worked the halyards. We stood six men on a watch, plus Jesse, who stood on my watch.

Jesse, I found out, was not an expert sailor, but he more than made up for it with his intense desire to win and his willingness to do anything within reason to accomplish that objective. He spends as much time worrying about and preparing for a race as anybody I know, and he's good at taking everybody else's advice and coming up with the right answer (something I think I'm good at also). On the boat, he is so positive that he can be *too* positive—sometimes he simply refuses to admit that the boat is doing badly. He's always asking questions, always pushing the crew, and always trying to get the best out of the boat. Even though he was the owner, it was understood that I was in charge, and whenever I was on deck I was *definitely* in charge.

When my adrenalin is really running, I can steer for two or three hours at a time, in a distance race, or perhaps for a five-hour day race, but I don't think I steer more than my share. I'm sometimes asked what makes a good helmsman, and I answer that a very experienced sailor who can concentrate can usually steer a boat well. The experience gives him the feel for when the boat is slowing down or has too much helm. And the concentration—on the jib tell tales and on waves—keeps him "on," with the correct amount of weather helm and correct angle to the wind. Although I like to be the guy in charge, I encourage feedback from the crew. Yet I don't like a lot of chitchat, and I want the suggestions to be in the form of questions. Someone might ask, "What do you think about taking the jib halyard up a little and moving the draft forward in the genoa?" I might simply nod, or I might say how much I want the halyard raised.

I work closely with my sail-trimmer when going to windward. He will have the jib sheet in his hand and a man on the coffee grinder to trim. He and I will know and trust each other, and when we're really sailing hard we'll work together well. If he knows I'm paying attention—and I'd better be—and if he sees the leeward tell tale on the jib flutter, he'll know that the sail is stalled and that he has to ease the sheet out a little either because I want to bear off to get through some bad waves or because the wind has lightened a little. If he sees the windward tell tale lift, that means that I want him to trim the genoa a bit because the wind has increased or because I can point a little higher in a patch of smooth water. I'll hear the sheet rubbing against the winch drum when it is eased or the click of the winch handle as it's trimmed, so I know what he's doing without him talking. So the sail-trimmer is more than just another crew member—in fact, he may be the second most important guy on deck.

One thing I've discovered is that if the crew on deck *thinks* that the helmsman is good, he *will* be good. They will try much harder for him because they want to look good in his eyes and because they want to make him continue to look good. If a helmsman has a good reputation, the odds are that the boat will go fast because everybody on board is making things easy for each other.

This close relationship between the sail-trimmer and the helmsman is just one of the things that makes racing boats larger than fifty feet so much different from racing a One Tonner. But there are other differences, too. With so many people, organization and logistics are vital: Who buys how much food? Where do you sleep the crew when the race is over? (There usually isn't that much room on board.) Are all the spinnakers stopped? Ashore, every time you want to get the whole crew together for a night out, it takes an hour to get everybody collected and cleaned up. The boat herself is so complicated, with a lot of plumbing and wiring, that maintenance can be a full-time job for somebody.

It's more difficult to race a big boat well, too. Since it takes two or three guys simply to get the genoas out of the forward hatch and on deck, a sail change is slower than it is on a One Tonner. Once you've made the change and folded up the old sail and settled down, if you decide that the old sail was better after all, you have second thoughts about changing back. If the crew works hard now, will they have enough energy left to work just as hard later on?

Since there are few big boats racing, they are often sailing with nobody else in sight. This makes it hard to sustain the same high that you have in a One Tonner or Two Tonner, when you can sail side-by-side with a bunch of boats for an entire race. With a couple of Two Tonners right next to your boat, you think twice before you go below to get a sandwich —it might slow your boat down. But if yours is the only boat around, you might (though you shouldn't) think nothing of having three guys gossiping in the cockpit. I think the ideal size for an ocean racer is a boat that you can sail hard and well with eight or nine people. A Two Tonner fits that requirement well, which may be why Two Tonners do so well. A forty-six-footer like *High Roler*, my boat for the 1977 SORC, is too large to race really well without a similar-sized boat alongside.

All of these were problems that I had to face for the first time in *Charisma*, and we were able to get matters pretty well sorted out during our spring sailing on Long Island Sound. A few guys sailed the boat over to England in July, and after the rest of the crew arrived, we spent a couple of days working on our speed and getting to know the area off the Isle of Wight. The Admiral's Cup consisted of four races, two day races in the Solent off Cowes, the Channel Race across to France and return, and the classic Fastnet Race to a rock off Ireland and back to Plymouth. The Solent is a tricky sailing area, with a lot of current, huge mud flats, and fluky wind. One calm day, we powered around the day-race course with the depth sounder on to see how close we could get to shore without running aground. We followed the eight-foot soundings at several tide levels (*Charisma* drew eight feet) so I could get a mental picture of the bottom's curvature. I have a good memory for things of that sort and for charts. In some areas there, only a couple of hours of tide can make a course difference of half a mile or more. I knew that I was weak on these problems and their solutions, so I spent more time working on them than anybody else there.

The Admiral's Cup has its eccentricities. Not only is it sailed in a place where local knowledge means so much, it has a peculiar starting line and some odd rules. One end of the

line is the Royal Yacht Squadron, with an inner restraining
mark that is in only six feet of water at low tide. The outer
mark is so far out that you have to be in the middle of the line
in order to read the course signals flown ashore at the squadron. Even then, if we wanted to start at the outer end, we had
to power at 7 1/2 knots after reading the course signals in
order to arrive before the preparatory gun.

Charisma was the second largest boat, rating 40.1 under the
IOR. *Tenacious*, with Ted Turner, rated 38.7, and *Robin*, with
Ted Hood, rated 32. Of the three skippers, only Turner had
sailed there before in an Admiral's Cup. Neither Hood nor
Turner is the most organized guy in the world, so I wasn't
sure how we would do. The English bookies had the British
and German teams as co-favorites, at 3–1 odds. The Australians were 5–1 and we were 6–1.

The first race was the Channel Race from Cowes to a
tower in the Channel, to Le Havre, and back to Cowes. I was
very conservative at the start since one of the peculiar rules
of the series was that you were disqualified if you were over
early. In the tune-up race, I had pushed Turner over early and
we had gone on to win. Al Van Metre, the team captain, was
really angry after the race and told us, "Six months from now
nobody will care who crossed the line first between you two
guys." And Turner said, "I'll remember!"

We had a mediocre start, but before long we were leading
the fleet. After a while, a British destroyer came alongside and
hailed us, and I had a sinking feeling and thought, "Damn!
We were over the line early and they're here to tell us."
Somebody on the destroyer hailed us and said to wave if we
heard him. We waved. Then somebody hailed, "Is there a Mr.
Kip Lewis aboard?" We waved—Kip was grinding a winch.

"Sorry to have a little bit of bad news for you," they said,
"but your wife is gravely ill. We've been asked to evacuate
you immediately so you can fly to the United States."

They lowered a rubber boat and came over. Kip, scared to
death, jumped in with his sea bag, the rubber boat went a

little distance away, and a helicopter took off from the destroyer, hovered over the boat, pulled Kip right up, and flew off toward shore. We later found out that he went right back to the airport—no passport, no ticket—and flew straight home Fortunately, his wife recovered.

After this temporary delay, we shook off our shock and got going again. We sailed well all night with *Bumblebee 3*, a very fast Australian fifty-one-footer, until we got near the French shore. But there we got lost. We had three navigators on board—Halsey Herreshoff, Pete Lawson, and an Englishman whom Jesse brought on for local knowledge—and each was giving different advice. We eventually agreed that we were about twelve miles off the coast, so we reached into shore and finally found the buoy in the fog, losing about an hour. Of course, the boats behind us had an advantage since they knew that we were coming from the turning mark as we passed them, but still we did well, as did Hood and Turner. The American team was leading the series.

Unfortunately, our lead did not survive the first day race, which was one of the strangest yacht races that I have ever sailed in. It started out well enough, with *Charisma* right with *Bumblebee* at the first mark in the West Solent and *Robin* and *Tenacious* in good positions behind us. But there was a different breeze in the East Solent, with a big calm patch in the middle. We sailed into the calm and ate our guts out for twenty minutes while everybody behind us caught up and *Bumblebee 3* got into the new breeze and shot ahead to a two-mile lead. Then we got into the new breeze and sailed away from the smaller boats. But we had to return through the calm, and the same thing happened all over again. Through all the confusion, the three United States boats were still doing pretty well, all in the top half-dozen boats or so.

The last bit was against a fast current. We beat up the shore to stay out of it, but had to round a buoy that was right out in the flow before going to the finish. This meant that we had to time our tack well—if we tacked too early, the current would push us well to leeward of the buoy. So we crept up the shore, well beyond the buoy, and tacked to fetch (we hoped) the mark so we could tack around it and head back to shore. But nobody made it—we were all swept to leeward. *Charisma* was making four knots through the water, but even that wasn't enough. Pretty soon, people started to slip their anchors over the side and for hour after hour we all sat there within a few hundred yards of the finish, waiting for the tide to change or for the wind to increase. It was the weirdest thing I've ever seen afloat.

Finally, an Argentinian boat, *Red Rock*, shot in on a little puff, tacked—and made the buoy—then an English boat, *Yeoman XX*. They finished hours ahead of the rest of us. The guys on *Bumblebee 3* got so frustrated that they tacked too early, hit the buoy, and had to drop out. When the tide finally changed, we all rounded together at 10 P.M. *Charisma* was thirty-eighth on corrected time, *Tenacious* was thirty-second, and Hood, who ran aground, was even worse. It was a disaster for the United States team.

Next was a straight-forward race in which we did well, and then the Fastnet Race. We had a perfect start, Halsey hit the Fastnet Rock lighthouse right on, and we rounded it like it was a mark in a buoy race, with waves throwing spray all over. There was a big calm off the Scilly Islands on the way back and the little boats caught up—it certainly was a small-boat event—but the United States team ended up third in the series, behind the English and the Germans. It was an interesting experience, but I was not happy either with the Admiral's Cup, which should be better run, or with our performance (although all the light, fluky air did not help the bigger boats).

Jesse asked me back aboard *Charisma* for the 1976 SORC. We sailed against *Bumblebee 3* again, and she was even faster. Our high point was winning the Lipton Cup with the starting tactic that we had used in *Stinger* in 1975—sailing down the Florida shore to get out of the current—and had a chance at winning Class A going into the Miami-Nassau Race. But we broke our mast in heavy air after the upper shroud snapped due to vibration and, of course, didn't finish. That ended my *Charisma* days.

CHAPTER 9

High Roler *in 1977*

BY THE end of the summer of 1976, I was exhausted, having spent most of the year either in *Charisma* on the SORC or in my Tempest, trying out for and sailing in the Olympics. People who say that sailing is not an active sport such as football or track have never spent months preparing a boat, a crew, and themselves for a major event like the Olympics. It is tiring (and expensive) work. Between the end of the Olympics in July and January, 1977, I think I sailed in only two races.

During that time, Jesse Philips had been in touch with me about sailing *Charisma* once again in the 1977 Circuit, but I kept putting him off, either because I was so tired of racing or because I had the idea that I might want to sail my own boat in Florida. Sitting in Carl Eichenlaub's yard was the half-completed hull of an aluminum forty-six-footer that Doug Peterson had designed. It had been commissioned by an East Coast sailor, who eventually decided that he did not want to get a new boat. Then an Italian marine hardware company became interested in the design and commissioned Eichen-laub to build the boat. After she was plated, however, they backed out. Carl put a deck on, and there the boat sat. I was lured by the hull. It looked like a good design for upwind sailing and, since 1977 would be an Admiral's Cup year, I thought I might sail in the Circuit and try to make the United States team. But there was no way that I could afford to pay for the whole boat, whose expense with rigging and sails would be close to two hundred thousand dollars, so I started looking around for partners.

I met Bill Power in September, and when somebody mentioned the idea of going in together on the boat, he seemed interested. Bill was a retired health-plan executive from Newport Beach who had sailed successfully in his Swan 44, *Questar*. He had caught the ocean racing bug and he wanted to give one serious try at the big time. We found quickly that we could work together since he was very good at organization. Carl finished the boat off beautifully, and she was launched at Thanksgiving with the name of *High Roler* (everybody plays a role; this boat would be successful and play a "high role"). We put together an excellent crew, despite the late date, did some tuning, and shipped the boat to New Orleans. Ben Mitchell, who was navigator, then sailed her through a blizzard across the Gulf of Mexico to St. Petersburg.

Since this was an Admiral's Cup year, there were a lot of new boats in the forty- to fifty-foot range, and these contenders for the three places on the American team would be sailed by some of the very best people. The boat I feared the most was Pat Haggerty's *Bay Bea*, a forty-six-footer, partly because she was a blown-up version of a One Tonner called *Resolute Salmon*, a Brit Chance-designed daggerboarder that had won the 1976 One Ton World Championship, but mainly because Dick Deaver would be on board (Dick had been *Resolute Salmon*'s skipper). This might be a replay of the 1975 SORC, with me and Deaver match-racing throughout the series, only in Class A boats rather than in One Tonners. Another new

Conner aboard *High Roler*, with co-owner Bill Power steering. *(Photo by John Rousmaniere.)*

High Roler in the 1977 SORC, in which she won Class A in the division for new boats. Here, Conner steers *High Roler* to windward. *(Photo by Bahamas News Bureau.)*

boat that many people thought would do well was a forty-eight-footer named *Scaramouche*, designed by German Frers. Her owner, Chuck Kirsch, had been successful with other boats having the same name, but I somehow felt—mistakenly, as it later turned out—that she would not be a problem.

We had never sailed *High Roler* in a good breeze off San Diego, and the first race, from St. Petersburg south to Boca Grande and return (replacing the old Anclote Key Race), showed me that we had a weakness in fresh air, especially when reaching. The Boca Grande Race started with a reach south in moderate to fresh air, and we soon blew *Scaramouche* right off while we covered *Bay Bea*. She could raise her daggerboard off the wind and reduce her wetted surface, but we kept up fairly well. On the beat back, we continued to move well on her until she withdrew because of a broken mast step. As it turned out, we paid too much attention to her, let several boats get to the right of us in a veering wind, and finished fifth in class. There were no official fleet standings, but, unofficially, we finished a poor 14th in the division of new boats.

After this inauspicious opener, we started the most important race, from St. Petersburg to Ft. Lauderdale. This is the race that, two years earlier, put *Stinger* in the lead to stay, but we weren't so fortunate this year. We had a good position at Rebecca Shoals and, in light beating, soon sailed right up on *Charisma*, which was some six feet larger, and left *Scaramouche* behind. But *Bay Bea* was gaining on us, even though we owed her about an hour in time. We eventually worked away from *Bay Bea* as we did what is normally the right thing by sailing moderately far out into the Gulf Stream, but the boats that were inshore—*Scaramouche* and *Charisma* especially—did a lot better; we ended up with another fifth in class. The top two places in the class and (unofficially) in the fleet were taken by two seventy-nine-foot ketches, *Kialoa* and *Ondine*, which had very little of the light beating that the smaller boats had. *Kialoa* finished two hours ahead of *Ondine*, which finished sixteen hours ahead of the next boat. *Charisma*, in fourth, corrected out only a minute ahead of us, but well behind *Scaramouche*, in third. It wasn't until after this race that I discovered that Ted Hood had been sailing in *Scaramouche*, with Chuck Kirsch, who himself is very good. Hood sailed in her for the rest of the Circuit. The racing was so mixed up by this stage that with two fifths we were still first in class, ahead of *Scaramouche* (with a tenth and a third) and *Charisma* (with a seventh and a fourth). The top boats in the first race, all forty-six-footers designed by German Frers, were way down in the Lauderdale race.

The boat's relative tenderness hurt us in the Ocean Triangle's early going, as we had to shorten down to a number three jib while *Scaramouche* drove away from us with her number one genoa up in about 16 knots of true wind. But it soon lightened up and got shifty and, hitting the headers just right, we soon passed *Scaramouche* and were fourth around the Great Isaac light. We next had a hard spinnaker beam reach across to the Florida shore. *High Roler* was so tender that it was extremely hard to keep her up to course without broaching. After half an hour, my arms got so tired that I asked Conn Findlay to come back and steer. I don't think he had steered a racing boat before, but he seemed a likely candidate since he was the strongest man on board, and a very experienced sailor. He did an excellent job. Unfortunately, our navigation was off, and we closed on Florida about ten miles too far to the south, had to take in the chute, and hardened up, losing a lot of boats to finish fifth. *Charisma*, which had been way back, ended up sixth, *Bay Bea* beat us for the first time in the series, and *Scaramouche* finished third behind two Frers 46s and was now first in our class. This was the low point of the SORC for me.

The fourth race was the Lipton Cup, starting with a beat up the Florida coast from Miami. Hood, in *Scaramouche*, had a beautiful port-tack start at the favored end and headed right out to the Gulf Stream's north-bound current. In about 15 knots of wind, he led us to the Ft. Lauderdale buoy. From

ST. PETERSBURG—BOCA GRANDE

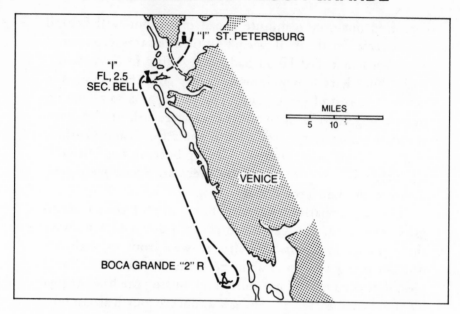

ST.PETERSBURG—FT. LAUDERDALE RACE

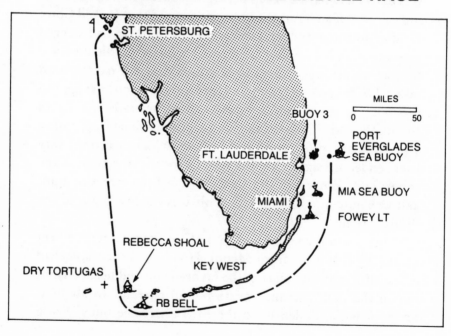

OCEAN TRIANGLE RACE

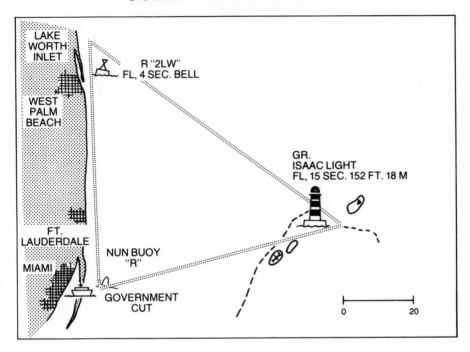

LIPTON CUP RACE

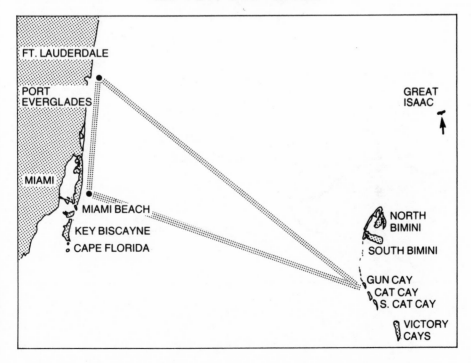

MIAMI—NASSAU RACE

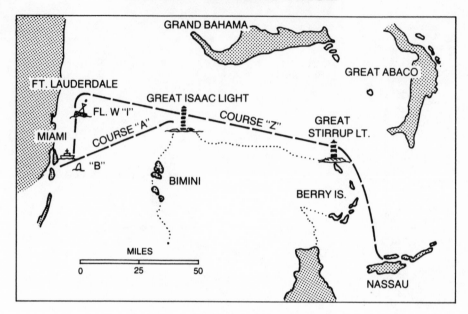

NASSAU CUP RACE

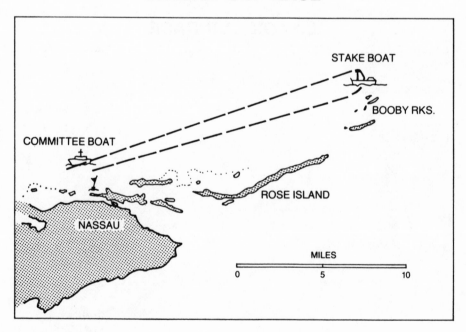

there, we had to sail across the Stream to Gun Cay, and since the breeze died a little, it seemed that the right thing to do was to sail south down the Florida shore inside the current, and then cut across to the cay. The only boat that did not do this was *Ondine*, which ended up winning the race. We and *Scaramouche* did it, with us cutting across before she did, but since the leg turned into another hard reach, in which we were weak, *Scaramouche* opened up on us by five minutes. The leg from Gun Cay to Miami turned into a light-air run, and we sailed well and caught *Scaramouche* to take third in our class. We were now one point ahead of *Scaramouche*.

Everything now came down to the Miami-Nassau Race, since whoever did best in it would have to do very poorly in the short Nassau Cup Race in order to lose his lead. *Bay Bea* was out of it because of her first-race breakdown, *Charisma* had faded, and the Frers 46s and the seventy-nine-footers had been extremely inconsistent, either winning or finishing back in the teens. So it was us and *Scaramouche*. We were hoping for light and moderate air, especially windward work, and they were hoping for fresh air, especially reaching.

We had an excellent start, they had a poor one, and in the light beat up to the Ft. Lauderdale mark before turning east we did well. Fortunately for us, the wind veered and we had a close reach and then a beat across the Stream in light air and choppy water. One guy in each of our watches was instructed never to take his eyes off of *Scaramouche*, because it was important that we never let her get away. We both ended up going the right way and finished one-two in our division and in fleet, with us a solid forty minutes ahead. We had all but clinched our class win and, perhaps, an Admiral's Cup berth. If *Scaramouche* won the Nassau Cup Race, we had to finish worse than fourth for her to win the series. Early in the light beat, we had a good boat-for-boat lead, but the wind came up and she caught us to take the race; but we finished safely in third, so we won our division and ended up fourth overall.

Unfortunately, by this time it looked as though we would

High Roler is a racing boat, with no cruising amenities. *(Photo by John Rousmaniere.)*

not be able to go to England after all. Bill Power had other interests and could not take the time, and I could not afford to pay the entire tab. I looked around unsuccessfully for a suitable partner and then, with some regret, told the Admiral's Cup selection committee that *High Roler* would be unable to go. (They ended up chosing *Scaramouche*, a forty-footer called *Imp* that had dominated Class B, and *Bay Bea*, despite her breakdown.)

I had some doubts about *High Roler*'s suitability for England, where it can blow hard, and in any case I wanted to get back to small boats again and be available for one of the 12-Meters working toward the 1977 America's Cup trials. Lowell North was in charge of a new Sparkman & Stephens design, *Enterprise*; Ted Hood was sailing his own design, *Independence*; and Ted Turner was back, this time in *Courageous*. The man who had bought *Intrepid* from the Seattle Sailing Foundation, Paul Fendler, had several times asked me to sail her, but he ran into financial difficulties and was forced to sell her and she ended up not going to Newport after all. I bought an old Star boat, and went back to where I started. I did well in spring regattas, won the North Americans, and headed to Europe for the Worlds.

An offer to sail in one of the United States Twelves did not materialize—because the three skippers understandably wanted to feel that they were in complete charge of their boats. In mid-August, however, when I was preparing for the Star World Championship, in Kiel, Germany, I was contacted by the backers of *Enterprise*, which had been beaten regularly by the surprising Ted Turner in *Courageous*. They asked me to sail as tactician under Malin Burnham, whom they had made skipper after relieving Lowell North. Although I had great respect for Malin and was really tempted to take up the offer, I said no since there was no indication that I could significantly help *Enterprise* win selection. I stayed with the Star boat and went

High Roler broad reaching in the Nassau Cup Race. *(Photo by Bahamas News Bureau.)*

on preparing for the Worlds, which I won easily, finishing first in five races. *Enterprise* was soon eliminated in the trials, and Ted Turner and *Courageous* went on to defend the Cup against Alan Bond's *Australia*.

IV

One-Design Racing

CHAPTER *10*

How to Win a Championship

So FAR I have talked mainly about racing big boats—12-Meters in the America's Cup and Cup trials and ocean racers in the SORC and Admiral's Cup—but in this and the following two chapters, we will look at what it takes to win championships in small boats. Just as with preparing *Courageous*, *Stinger*, and *Charisma* for a big series, getting a one-design boat like a Star or a Tempest ready for a North American Championship or an Olympic Games requires strict attention to the boat, to the crew, and to your own mental attitude. If you do all of that correctly, the odds are good that you will be in the top five in your class, all other things (such as sailing experience) being equal. After that, a "no risks" approach on the race course, luck, and attention to detail may combine to make you number one.

Let's assume that you are interested in racing a Lightning —although the approach I'm about to describe will work in any one-design class. Your first problem is selecting a boat. Plan to start where everybody else is. Visit a major championship, talk to the sailmakers and the hot people in the class, and read the class newsletter—all with the goal of finding out what requipment is winning. If one builder and one sail-maker are doing consistently well, then buy their best boat and sails and set them up exactly the same way that a top guy with that equipment is doing. Determine his mast rake by hauling a tape measure up his main halyard and measuring the distance between the masthead and the middle of his transom. Find his mast position by measuring the base of his foretriangle. Then put your mast in exactly the same position. We do this all the time in the Star Class, and I can remember Valentin Mankin, the Russian Tempest sailor, going to the effort of using a strain gauge to determine the tension on the diamond shrouds of John Albrechtson's boat at the Olympics. If Valentin, a two-time gold-medal winner, has the humility to duplicate the tune of a boat that is beating him, then a sailor new to a class should be able to copy a champion.

As you will see in the next chapter, that is how I prepared my Tempest when I first bought it in the fall of 1975. Knowing what the good guys were doing meant that I had a foundation of knowledge upon which to experiment, one change at a time. Another good sailor who joined the Tempest Class at about the same time did things entirely differently. He had a yacht designer create a differently-shaped keel. He had an expert completely refinish the hull. He used carbon-fiber masts. He experimented with rake and mast position. These were all great ideas, but if the boat was going either very fast or very slow, he would have had no idea which innovation was responsible. If he had started where everybody else in the class was, he would have used his time and energy much more constructively.

You have bought a stiff boat that is light in the ends and you have set it up the way the good skippers are doing it. You should now work hard to get the hull just as fair as possible. There will be all sorts of hollows and bumps that can be faired out using wet-or-dry sandpaper on a two-foot board or piece of Styrofoam plastic foam. Keep sanding with increasingly fine sandpaper until the hull is fair. Lowell North doesn't trust his eye here; he uses a very sensitive scale that can measure hollows and rises. Make sure that the rudder and centerboard or keel are the optimum shape. Often, they are asymmetrical and need building up with microballoons. Finally, give the bottom, rudder, and centerboard or keel a good sanding with four-hundred-grit wet-or-dry sandpaper. Some people like to add a coating of Teflon fluorocarbon resins or soap, but class rules often prohibit this and, in any case, the coating usually washes off within a couple of hours.

Next, do a lot of sailing with a tune-up boat. One-on-one sailing is the best way to develop boat speed. One boat remains constant while the other makes changes in trim, leads, or sail shape one at a time. The sailmaker should go out with you a few times. Once you're sure that the sails are right, set the outhaul, Cunningham, jib leads, and mast bend the way the sailmaker recommends and then work hard to find the correct sheet tension for different wind velocities. In most classes, the difference between the guys who go fast upwind and the guys who go *very* fast is in the main sheet tension. The boat's balance and the behavior of tell tales on the main's leech and on the sail itself will tell you a lot, but how you do against the tune-up boat will tell you even more. Make sure that you mark the controls and sheets, using different color marking pens for different conditions.

The tune-up boat should be the fastest one you can find. For instance, in San Diego there is a sailmaker who works for Lowell North named Pete Bennett. He rarely wins big Star boat championships even though he can make a Star go faster than can anybody else in the world. So before a North Americans or an Olympic Trials, I want to be able to sail against Pete as much as I can to work on boat speed. The wind is very steady off San Diego, so we sail on one tack for a couple of hours, making tiny changes and seeing how they affect speed. Most other champion sailors have favorite tuning partners, though some, like Buddy Melges in the Soling and Ding Schoonmaker in the Star, somehow seem able to do well tuning alone.

While you are tuning, you should be thinking about sail-handling gear. Of course, the type and location of many cleats, hiking straps, and other equipment will depend to a great extent on both your crew's personal preferences and the skipper's idiosyncracies. I have several preferences. One is that I like to have gadgets to fool around with. On the Tempest, I rigged remote control jib leads, even though I figured that I would change the leads very rarely, if ever. But I wanted that capability. Another preference of mine is to make the main sheet as short as possible by eliminating parts. On *Stinger*, my One Tonner, we had a one-part sheet that led to a winch. We could trim and ease it quickly and because there were no extra parts there was less stretch than usual. My Tempest had a five-part main sheet instead of the six parts that everybody else had, and my Star main sheet now has one part. This means I can pull in less line at mark roundings. I also had a one-part traveler control on the Tempest because I wanted to be able to make quick adjustments to the traveler without having to pull or ease all the line that a two- or three-part control would have. Another thing I worry about is the cleat I am using for a job. There are many types of cam and clam cleats on the market, and each is good for a particular duty.

While you are preparing the hull and rig, you should be thinking about your crew. One thing that always surprises me about people who say that they are really serious about sailing is how many of them sail only with their friends. The most basic mistake that most people make is that they choose their crews not for their size or ability but for their companionship. There are a lot of people who try to sail Stars with friends who weigh only 180 pounds, but it takes a strong 200-pounder wearing a lot of wet sweatshirts to hold down a Star in fresh air. Ron Anderson, my present Star crew,

weighs 250 pounds. I was surprised when I started sailing
Tempests that many people who had been in the class for
years were trying to get away with 190-pounders as crew. A
good Tempest crew will weigh at least 215, and John Albrechtson's man at the Olympics, Ingvar Hansson, must have
weighed 240. Friendship off the water can sometimes interfere with success on the water. It is sometimes hard for a
skipper to tell his friend, a crew member, what to do, and
equally hard for the crew to tell the skipper what he is doing
wrong.

While you are doing all this work in preparation for a big
championship, you don't want to tip your hand to the competition. In 1972, Alan Holt surprised the Star Class by winning
the Olympic Trials at San Francisco with a special heavy-
weather rig and sail that he had developed in Seattle. I ended
up fourth in the trials, but I might have won if I'd taken the
time and effort to trail my boat up to Seattle to sail against
Holt, assuming that he would have used that gear against me.
The really good sailors will wait until the eleventh hour before selecting their sails for a big series. They will see what
the sailmakers in the class are using or are working on in the
last couple of weeks before a championship and, if they can,
they will evaluate those sails against the ones they have been
using. Often the older sails are just as good or better, but
sometimes they are not.

So, a week before the championship, you have a boat as
good as everybody else's; you have reliable gear that fits your
personality; you have the best sails you can find on the best
mast available; you have a good strong crew with the correct
weight who won't let you down when the going gets tough;
and you know how to make your boat go fast. Almost auto-
matically, you should be in the top ten and maybe the top five.

Here's how you become number one.

You and your crew get to the regatta site at least three days
and preferably a week before the practice race. You check into
a comfortable place to stay, and then you rig your boat and

sail on the course for several hours every day. At first there probably won't be any other boats there, so you get the kinks out, practice spinnaker sets and jibes, and carefully study the local wind and current conditions. You pay a visit to the local airport to ask about weather, talk with some local sailors about special conditions, and take wind readings at the times when races will be held. You also check tide tables (if you are sailing in tidal waters) and take a look at buoys and moorings to see how the current runs.

When your competitors start to arrive, you spend as much time as you can tuning up against the good crews (who will of course be impressed by the fact that you arrived before they did). You measure in your boat and sails, make sure you have all the required safety gear, and then go over everything very carefully to make sure that cotter pins are in place and that nuts are not falling off of bolts.

The night before the first race you make sure that you and your crew stay sober and get to bed at a decent hour. When you wake up you have the slightly sick-to-the-stomach feeling that means you are ready. You are nervous, but not panicked, and you go down to the boat early, if only to be at the dock when everybody else arrives. People always seem to get upset when they think that the other guy is better prepared than they are.

You rig the boat and leave early enough so that you arrive at the line at least an hour before the first gun. That hour is not for relaxation. It's for finding out what the wind and current are doing, for getting your sails and trim right, and for getting your psych up. Start concentrating right away: check jib leads and halyard tension; find the right sheet tension; get going fast. Head into the wind every five minutes and write down the wind direction. Then sail close-hauled on both tacks and write those headings down, too. Check the headings on the reaches to see if you can carry a spinnaker.

When the other boats arrive, find the best one and go on

the wind against him. Since your trim is right and you are comfortable with the boat and the conditions, you will probably be faster. His leads or mast rake may be wrong, or he may still be eating lunch. After you blow him off for a very short time, bear off and sail away. You don't want to give him a chance to tune against you. You only want him to remember that you were faster than he was.

By now, your research coupled with any forecasts you may have received that morning from the airport will give you an idea which side, if any, of the beat is favored. You should also know which end of the line to start at. One way to tell is to sail straight down the line on starboard tack with the main trimmed perfectly. Then cleat the main, tack or jibe, and sail back down the line on port tack. If the main is luffing, the starboard end is favored. If the main can be eased, the port end is favored. And if the main is still trimmed perfectly, the line is square to the wind.

There are a lot of factors that you must consider while planning your start. One is the favored end. Getting the perfect start on a biased line can give you an immediate three- or four-boat length advantage. But remember that if you don't get that perfect start, you may be trapped in somebody else's backwind for a long time. Another thing to think about is that if you start at the port, or leeward, end of the line, it will be very difficult for you to get over to the right-hand side of the course on port tack without ducking a lot of sterns and losing a lot of distance. So, is that perfect leeward-end start worthwhile if the right is favored? A third consideration is that you are sailing a series, where consistency wins. High risk and high reward always go together, and over a six- or seven-race series, you want to minimize your risks. My preference is usually to avoid taking chances. I have enough confidence in myself, my boat, and my crew to know that I'm going to be in the top five boats unless I make a really bad mistake. Early in a series, if one end is really favored, I'll start about one-third of the way up from it, with clear air and good speed. Later in the series, if I need to win a race I might take the risk of a pin-end start.

With three minutes to go, I check the wind direction again and then work my way just to leeward of the port end. On port tack, I sail down the line toward the committee boat and the fleet approaching on starboard, looking for a good hole to tack into. The hole always will be there, and when I find it, I tack under the bow of the next boat up and squeeze him up a little, both to keep him from driving over me and to make a hole to leeward. If I see somebody on port tack trying to do the same thing to me, I head off a little to discourage him from tacking under my bow. With thirty seconds to go, I get my boat going by trimming my sails and footing off into the hole I made. Most people trim in too late, which is why there is almost always a big sag in the middle of the line.

Of course, sometimes you just have to get a perfect start if you want to win the series. I remember a start that Lowell North made in a Star World Championship in a race he had to win. He and Peter Barrett, his crew, came planing down the line toward the favored end. They were just over the line until about five seconds before the start, when they bore off to the correct side and then luffed across right at the buoy. Everybody else was still accelerating when they were going top speed, and they had a five-boat-length lead immediately. But I don't recommend that kind of start as standard procedure.

As soon as we're moving and off the line, I start thinking about wind shifts. Because I've studied the wind carefully for an hour before the start, I know if my heading is high or low of the average. If I want to go to the right on port tack, I wait for the first header, find a hole in the fleet off my windward quarter, and tack up through it.

If you don't have a side preference, you simply have to be alert to wind shifts as they come. Your crew can't always tell you when you have been lifted or headed, and the compass reacts too slowly. The best way to tell is by comparing your heading with that of boats around you. If you are getting closer to a boat to leeward, you're headed. If you are working up under a boat to windward, you're lifted. One rule is not to underestimate the people you're sailing against in the top level of your class. If you are heading lower or higher than they are, it's because you're headed or lifted or because something is a bit wrong with your sail trim. In general, people rely on the compass too much. It certainly helps tell you about lifts and headers when there is nobody else around, but if you're sailing in a group of boats, trust relative bearings as much as you rely on the compass.

Some people say that they can tell if the wind will head or lift them by watching the water ahead, but I'm dubious. Dark water ahead means a puff, and a puff almost always means a change in direction, but unless the puff is coming from one side or the other, I don't think you can tell much about the direction of the shift. If you are sailing in an off-shore wind, you might be able to smell wind shifts. Valentin Mankin is a marvelous sailor, there is no question about it, but if he can smell shifts in an onshore southwesterly wind at Kingston, as he claims, I'll be surprised. What he can do, though, is see boats up ahead that have big headers and lifts, and he can see a puff coming from way on the left that will lift him on port tack and head him on starboard tack.

On the first part of this beat, you should be making your boat go as fast as you can while you think about shifts and keep your air clear. Don't tack too often, unless the wind is really shifty; just exploit the speed advantage that you have after all your preparation. About two-thirds of the way up the beat, you have an idea which side is paying off the best, and you have probably gone off part of the way to that side. Don't go all the way to the lay line, since the wind may shift back —just far enough to cover your losses. Assuming now that you have done all of this and that the wind has not been too shifty, the odds are very good that you are at least fifth at the weather mark. The guys ahead of you may be there because one of them got the perfect start, because one of them played a shift perfectly, and because two more, like you, sailed a fast, conservative leg and deserve to be there. Now you are in an excellent position to pick up some boats and maybe win the race.

The first decision you face after rounding the mark and setting the spinnaker is whether to sail on or high of the rhumb line to the jibe mark. In some classes, people are tempted to sail high under jib alone until they get clear air, and then set the spinnaker and bear off. In a planing boat, this may pay off, since the most windward boat will get puffs first and, in marginal planing conditions, be able to kick off on a wave and accelerate rapidly by boats to leeward. In a heavy boat like a Lightning, however, those boats are often sailing a needlessly long course. Tom Allen used to pick up a lot of boats on reaches in that class by bearing off to the course and setting his spinnaker as soon as he rounded. You may have to sail high of the rhumb line after rounding to discourage a boat that is trying to drive over you, but often you will beat him anyway just by sailing a short, fast course. Another advantage to staying low is that you will be on the inside at the jibe mark.

With good technique and sail trim, you can gain fantastic amounts of distance off the wind—sometimes a minute or two a leg. If there are waves, the racing rules allow you to pump the sails and "ooch" your body around to promote surfing and planing. This is where the crew pay their way with good spinnaker trimming and alertness to waves. Before you get to the jibe mark, you have to decide whether you can carry the spinnaker on the next reach. If you have doubts, you can lower the spinnaker and reset it on the next leg, and, most of the time, the boats astern will follow suit. But a really aggressive skipper with a good crew will usually try to carry and drive over you just after the jibe, and you will have to be ready to luff hard to close him off. In a boat like a Lightning, the two crew members can handle the sails and keep the boat flat while the skipper concentrates on tactics and steering. But in a two-man spinnaker boat like a 470 or a Tempest, both people have their hands full all the time. For instance, after a jibe I steered the Tempest with one foot, hiked with the other foot, and trimmed the spinnaker and the mainsail with both hands while Conn Findlay put the pole on the mast. There wasn't much I could do about tactics then.

On the way down the second reach, you will have a lot to do just to keep the boat moving fast and your air clear. But you should be thinking carefully about the upcoming windward leg. Which side paid off the first time up? Has the wind shifted during the reaches? Is the current the same? If you're finding it hard to carry the chute on this second reach on port tack, that means that you're headed. That also means a starboard tack lift. Since you should sail the lifted tack, you should plan on tacking just after you round the mark. If this is what you decide, make sure that your crew knows it so he won't be surprised. Whatever your decision, make up your mind before the rounding because there will be a lot of other things to worry about then: get the spinnaker down, put the pole away, clean up the sheets, tension the Cunningham and the backstay, lower the centerboard, set the jib leads. You're going to forget to do at least one of those things until you're half-way around the mark. As soon as you are around and settled down, compare the compass reading with your memory of what the wind did on the first beat.

You're in third place now, since the boat that made the perfect start sailed too high on the first reach and you drove through his lee, and one of the other boats blew the jibe. Six boat lengths ahead in first place is Bill Shore, who has won a Lightning World Championship and a couple of North Americans, so you know he's going to be hard to catch. Just a length ahead of you is Matt Fisher, a young Ohio sailor who has won a North Americans. Three lengths behind you in fourth is boat number 12,000, whose skipper you have never seen before, and two lengths behind him in fifth is Bruce Goldsmith, another former world champion.

Although this is the first race, you know that Shore and Goldsmith are the guys to beat in the series, that Fisher should do well, and that number 12,000 is an unknown. The important thing here is to make sure that the boats ahead don't get too far away and that the boats behind don't catch you while you're worried about the boats ahead. Shore, in first place, rounded the mark very intelligently. He sailed a couple of boat lengths (half the distance between him and Fisher), tacked to starboard, and then tacked back to port just before Fisher rounded. This put him in an excellent covering position, with both boats on port. You tack immediately after rounding, partly to get clear air but mainly because of the port tack header you discovered on the second reach. You now have a chance to catch Fisher since he does not tack. But since number 12,000 and Goldsmith stay on port after rounding, after a while you tack back to port yourself, even though the wind hasn't shifted back. It's just too risky to get far away from the competition and, anyway, you may already have caught Fisher by sailing on the lifted tack for a couple of minutes. Goldsmith is the guy you're really worried about, yet the last thing you want to do is to tack on his wind. If you do that, he'll tack to clear his air and force you to decide between covering him and sailing near Fisher. If this were a race late in the series and you were fighting for the series lead with one or a combination of these four boats, you might do any of a number of things. For instance, if it were important either to win the race or to beat Shore, you would probably hold on starboard, the lifted, tack. But early in the series, with this beat and a run to go, you play the percentages, trust your boat speed, and don't take any major chances.

Just after you tacked to port, the wind swung left 5 degrees to lift you, and now you are about three boat lengths to windward and almost abeam of Fisher, and seven boat lengths dead to windward of 12,000 and Goldsmith. You are now in second, only three lengths behind Shore, who is dead ahead. What should you do? You know that Shore won't tack until you or Fisher do, and you are pretty sure that Fisher won't tack until he's been headed and has a chance of starboard-tacking you. So you drive off just a little bit, footing for the port-tack header that should come and trying to stick your bow out in front of Fisher's, so that when the header comes your losses are minimized. This is tricky, because you don't want to sail into Shore's bad air, but if it doesn't work you can always start pointing again. To do this, sail with the leeward jib tell tale dancing a little bit every now and then—you don't have to ease anything.

Soon, everybody is headed 5 degrees. Fisher and Shore tack and you are just able to cross Fisher before tacking yourself in a covering position. Behind, Goldsmith tacks, but number 12,000 tacks right on him and Goldsmith has to go back the other way. Except for the possibility that Goldsmith will find some new wind over on the right, you're sitting pretty.

The question you ask yourself now is, "Should I go after Shore?" It's tempting—you could tack on the first tiny header, split with Shore and Fisher, and go wind-hunting over on the right with Goldsmith. But if that "header" was only wishful thinking (as it often is) and if starboard tack stays lifted, you could lose two boats—Fisher and 12,000. Remember that Goldsmith probably is only trying to keep his wind clear by getting away from 12,000. More important, remember that this is only the first race. Why not be satisfied with a second? So you resist the temptation to split with the leaders and keep a loose cover on Fisher all the way to the second weather mark. Coming into the mark on starboard, still three lengths behind Shore, you are three lengths abeam and to windward of Fisher; two lengths astern of him is Goldsmith. If this were a late race and if the scores were close, it might be important to try to get Goldsmith between you and Fisher, and then you would try to drive Fisher back by covering him tightly. Another score situation might require Fisher to finish between you and Goldsmith, so you would do nothing.

In any case, having tacked onto the starboard tack layline about twenty-five yards from the mark, you see that the wind has swung right 7 degrees and you are lifted. This indicates that you might overstand and that, though he won't catch you, Fisher will gain a little—bad news—but it also means that Shore, whose crew has set the spinnaker pole to starboard, will be on the wrong jibe after he rounds—good news. Starboard jibe will take him away from the finish; port jibe will take you toward the finish. You tell your crew to get ready for a jibe-set, and they have just enough time to get the sheets and halyard set up. You bear off at the mark, jibe, and hoist the chute.

As soon as Shore sees your jibe-set, he jibes, but he has already lost a third of his lead because of the extra distance he has sailed. You pay careful attention to the compass and as soon as you see that you are lifted, you jibe to starboard (upwind, tack in the headers; downwind, jibe in the lifts). In a way you have the advantage now, because you are the trailing boat and can take the initiative and attack.

But you must remember that this isn't a match race. Fisher and Goldsmith are just behind you, and they can do to you what you're going to Shore. In a match race, you would try to jibe back and forth across Shore's stern, taking his wind each time and slowing the race down to give you more time to catch him. But with two other boats to worry about, here you can only try to sail the shortest distance at the greatest speed. Since Shore can do the same thing, he wins the race, with you second, Fisher third, and Goldsmith fourth. It's almost impossible for Shore to win every race, and the next time you'll have your chance.

I have emphasized attitude in this chapter because it has a lot to do with success on the race course. If you want to know more details about starting techniques or sail trim or tactics, there are a lot of good books and articles available.

Some of the best are the oldest: Arthur Knapp's *Race Your Boat Right* and Stanley Ogilvy's *Thoughts on Small Boat Racing* are two of them. But no amount of reading will win races for you. Hard work, determination, open-mindedness, self-confidence, and attention to detail will get you going in the right direction and keep you going, too.

CHAPTER 11

The Olympic Trials

SOMETIME IN the summer of 1975, I decided that I wanted to win an Olympic gold medal in Canada in 1976. I really enjoyed small-boat sailing, but had done very little of it since finishing fourth in the Star Olympic Trials in 1972 and ninth in the World Championship in 1973. Since then, the America's Cup and ocean racing had taken all of my energy and time.

The problem was that the boat I knew the best, the Star, was no longer an Olympic class, so I had to choose between six classes about which I knew either nothing or very little. Since no matter which class I chose, I would be years behind the leaders in experience and knowledge, it was important to get going as soon as I could. The Olympic classes attract some of the best sailors in the world. Many are professional sail or hardware makers who can justify putting a lot of time and money into their sailing, even in non-Olympic years. And here I was, a San Diego businessman. But since the Olympics are the top of the small-boat world, the challenge was irresistible.

The six Olympic classes for 1976 were the Finn, the 470, the Flying Dutchman, the Tornado, the Soling, and the Tempest. I had sailed Finns, singlehanded centerboarders, and knew that they demanded much better physical conditioning than I had. Anyway, I liked having somebody to talk to in the boat. The 470 is a small two-man centerboarder. If the crew weight is more than about 260 pounds, the boat isn't competitive, which meant that I would have to find a good 60-pound crew. So the 470 was out. The Flying Dutchman, a larger two-man centerboarder that could use a normal-sized crew, was interesting, as was the Tornado, a catamaran. But I didn't know much about either type of boat.

So I was left with the Soling and the Tempest. The Soling is a three-man keelboat that has some of the best sailors in the world. Since the United States had the strongest Soling fleet, with Buddy Melges, Bill Buchan, John Kolius, and some others, and since my priority was to make the United States team and win a medal, I reluctantly said no to the Soling. By process of elimination, I ended up with the Tempest. But, actually, the Tempest was the best boat for me, considering my skills and background. It is a twenty-two-foot keelboat that is in many ways similar to the Star, although it has a spinnaker and a trapeze. Of course, Lightning sailing had taught me a lot about spinnakers, and the trapeze didn't seem too complicated. In addition the United States fleet, which had been at the top of the world in the early 1970s, was now relatively weak, so it looked like I had a good shot at winning the Tempest Olympic Trials and making the team at Kingston, Ontario. On my way to England for the Admiral's Cup, I stopped off at the pre-Olympic regatta at Kingston, to look around. I went out to watch a race, asked some questions ashore, and bought two boats. I thought the two boats would be necessary so I would always have a tune-up boat for other Tempest crews or visiting guest experts to sail. Since I was starting so far behind everybody else, it was really important to use my time wisely.

After returning from the Admiral's Cup, I sailed one of the boats in the Tempest North American Championship, at Marblehead, Massachusetts. My crew was David McComb, an experienced Tempest sailor. This was the first time I had ever sailed, much less raced, a Tempest, but after some equipment and boat-handling problems were solved, I was happy to see that we were moving at least as fast as the best boats there. In one of the last races, we went extremely well against one boat and McComb started to get very excited. So did I when he told me that the crew sailing that boat, Glen Foster and Peter Dean, had won the Olympic bronze medal in 1972. We eventually finished second in the championship, beating Foster and several other very experienced people, although the Linville brothers and Argyle Campbell, who everybody said were the best Americans in the class, were not sailing. I had a friend trail the boats across the country to San Diego, and in October I started to get acquainted with this new class. Of course, I was encouraged by my performance at the North Americans. Picking a crew for the Tempest was hard because the guy had to be big and good. The Tempest has a lot of sail area, so you usually need a man who weighs over 225 pounds and who is at least 6′3″ tall. I thought immediately of Conn Findlay, whom I had sailed with in *Mariner* the year before. He was a good choice for other reasons besides his size. He had already won three Olympic medals—two gold and a bronze—in rowing, so he knew what an all-out winning effort was all about, and he wanted to do it. He was forty-five years old but in excellent condition. The only problem was that he hadn't sailed much in small boats and knew very little about flying a spinnaker. Still, a Tempest is a keelboat that is extremely difficult to capsize, and it is not a hard boat to move around in even for someone as large as Conn, who is about 6′4″ and 230 pounds.

We first sailed together around Christmas, 1975, against the Canadian Leibel brothers. They were using their sails on one of my boats and Conn and I used another boat. I could immediately tell that Conn's weight made a lot of difference, since I had been practicing with lighter crews.

At first we worked only on upwind boat speed and ignored boat-handling altogether. I got sails of different types from different sailmakers (although I probably could have got a discount if I had bought all my sails from one loft). We worked on sail controls and paid a lot of attention to our standing rigging. We installed jib leads that could be moved in and out by remote control to see how lead changes would affect speed. When we weighed the mast, we discovered to our horror that when we put the top of the spar on a scale, the weight of the tip was one pound over the minimum. One pound way up at the top of the mast can increase your heeling and pitching moment considerably. More important, knowing that the tip is so heavy can be a real psychological disadvantage (we used to worry about three ounces in the Stars). To get the tip weight down, I cut off the mast right to the top black band, made the shrouds as small as possible, eliminated the permanent backstay, and instead of using two bolts to hold the stays at the hounds I used one bolt. Eventually I got the tip weight down to minimum. I did all I could to get the boat right, but I still couldn't do everything I wanted since I had to go to Florida and sail the SORC in *Charisma*.

Although it may seem that I was going all-out on the Tempest, the uppermost thing in my mind in January and February was sailing the SORC. After that, in mid-March, there was the Congressional Cup, and then, finally, I would start racing the Tempest, first at the SPORT regatta at St. Petersburg just after the Congressional Cup and then at some important regattas in Europe. The Olympic Trials would be held in late June at the United States Sailing Center, on Association Island, near Watertown, New York. The Olympics—assuming I made the team—would be held at Kingston, Ontario, in late July. So I didn't have much time to get a good program going. I was beginning to feel a little bit like Ted Turner must, flying from one regatta to another.

During the SORC, Conn and I were able to get some time in against Don Cohan, sailing a borrowed boat, but it was SPORT (St. Petersburg Olympic Regatta for Training) that would tell us how competitive we were. Sailing there would be Jack and Jim Linville, brothers from Connecticut, and Argyle Campbell, from Newport Beach, California. The Linvilles had been sailing Tempests since the late sixties, had once won a World Championship, and almost always did well in international events. Campbell, who had done well in Snipes and who had won two Congressional Cups, had been sailing Tempests for five years and had been the number one United States boat in 1975. We hadn't sailed against each other, since neither had been at the North Americans in Marblehead, although I had hoped at one state that we might do some tuning. We were pretty fast and it was a close series for the first half. Then the Linvilles either sailed a little faster or a little better and won the series with us a close third behind a Canadian, Peter Nygard. Argyle was fourth, so we had beaten one very good boat. The series taught us that the Linvilles were going to be our toughest competition, but that they certainly would not be overpowering. Our crew work was not good and we didn't have the best sails, so we knew we could be competitive.

The next step of the program was to go to the European Championship in Italy. Several years before, the Americans had been the best in the Tempest Class, but by 1975 the Europeans were on top. It was important to sail against them to find out where we stood and to see what kind of gear they were using, early enough so we could do something about it. So I made arrangements to borrow a boat and I took my sails over. I had hoped to ship over one of my boats, but I couldn't find a convenient shipping route on short notice. It was quite easy to borrow a competitive boat, so I don't think we were at a disadvantage. The best hulls were built by Mader, a German company, and the best masts were made in England by Proctor, and it wasn't hard finding a boat with that combination. Campbell and Linville did the same thing, although I think that their equipment was a little better than ours since their hulls were new and mine was four years old. Anyway, we went to learn, not to win.

What we learned was that the Americans were so far out of it that the chances of our winning a medal were practically nil. At the European Championship, Conn and I were the first Americans by some bit—we were thirteenth, the Linvilles were eighteenth and Argyle was twenty-third in a sixty-boat fleet. But the twelve boats ahead of us were from nine different countries. Literally everyone who would be at the Olympics was there, even the Australian. It was a true pre-Olympic regatta as much as had been the one the year before at Kingston, which, of course, I had missed. It was an invaluable experience for me, and without it I would not have had as good a chance at winning the gold medal as I had.

When you go to a regatta like that and don't do very well, you still can use the event to help your sailing. The first thing you should do is to look carefully at all the other boats—especially at the ones that are doing very well—and make sure that your boat is set up the same way that they are, with the mast and the shrouds in the same place, with the same stay-tension, and with the same kind of sail-control equipment. You want to be able to go home with a fixed reference point that you can start off from in your tuning and practice. You just don't know how much you have to do to win until you sail against the best in the world and set your boat up the same way that they do.

Another thing we learned was that our sails weren't very good. They had been made in North's Connecticut loft, but now I ordered sails from the Elvstrom loft in Denmark and the North loft in Germany. So with new, competitive sails and an idea of how to rig the boat, we were starting pretty much from scratch with only a month or so until the Olympic Trials. We had taken care of one important and time-consuming job, however, and that was to fair the hulls of both my boats. Some of the best Europeans might have been able to get preferential treatment from Mader and be delivered hulls that were a little lighter in the ends. But I think I may have compensated for this by lightening or removing bow and stern fittings. In general, I thought that my hulls were at least equal to the best in the world.

In May, my program went into high gear. Even though I was discouraged by what I found in Europe, I took as positive an attitude as I could and came back to San Diego ready to make my equipment and myself as good as possible. I decided to use in the trials the German North sails when it was light and the Elvstrom sails when it was windy, and I know now that that decision was a turning point. Everybody else was using the American Norths except for Argyle Campbell, who had German sails and who ended up second in the trials. The Linvilles were limited by the fact that Jim Linville was a sailmaker at North in Connecticut. That's a good example of how professionalism can work against you, and of one advantage I have in not being a sailmaker. He would not use the German North sails, either because he was afraid of hurting his business in Connecticut or because he was prejudiced in favor of his own product. I came home and made my gear like everyone else's and took off some equipment. I had discovered that moving jib leads outboard when it got windy didn't seem to help, so I took the athwartships controls off and, like the good Europeans did, moved the leads aft when we started to get overpowered. Sometimes you can have too much gear, but one gadget that I had did help me sail the boat a little better. I wanted to be able to trim or ease the jib sheet by small amounts without Conn having to lean in from the trapeze. So we rigged up a three-to-one purchase on the jib sheet cleats, which slid on short tracks, so I could adjust the trim with one hand by moving the cleat. A jib on a Tempest is not easy to handle when it's windy, even by somebody as strong as Conn. Often when the crew makes the adjustment the sheet slips when he puts it back in the cleat, and by the time he gets the trim right again the wind velocity has changed and it's time to make another adjustment. The tackle permitted me to ease the sheet easily if I saw a particularly bad group of waves coming and then trim it back in when the water smoothed, without Conn moving. I also had one less part in the main-sheet and traveler than anybody else had, even the Europeans. Like the jib trim system, this probably had no great signifi-cance in my performance, and I almost certainly would have done just as well without it. But it made me feel more com-fortable in the boat. Knowing that my main sheet or my jib sheet or my mast was the best, made me that much more confident. I guess that I could do well in a boat if the gear were only half right, but why should I do it that way if I can make it perfect? It's just a matter of effort.

I had some carbon fiber spreaders made. They were lighter and stronger than the metal spreaders, but I decided not to use them. This was partly because the mast was mini-mum weight anyway and partly because I didn't want to take a chance on their breaking. But I did use solid bar stays and I faired up the mast and fittings with putty, which were things that only one other Tempest sailor, Don Cohan, did. So along with the excellent hull, I had a really superior rig. And I knew that I had the best sails.

Going into the trials, I felt pretty confident, and I knew that if I won I had a good chance against John Albrechtson, the Swede who had been the best in the world during the previous six months. Albrechtson was a professional sail-maker for Elvstrom, so he, too, could not use the German North sails in light air.

We were the first Tempest crew to arrive at the United States Olympic Trials, a week before everybody else started coming in and a couple of weeks before the series began. We worked hard on our boat-handling until we could tack the boat and set the spinnaker well. When the other boats turned up, we saw that we had the best hull there, although a couple of boats had better-shaped keels and rudders. I was on a pretty big high and felt I could beat everybody there except possibly the Linvilles, who showed the best speed in the practice race. We already knew from some racing and tuning-up in California that we could beat Argyle Campbell.

With the Linvilles the one to beat, we just went the same way they did off the first start. It was the wrong way, and we were eighth to their eleventh at the first mark, and gained all through the race to finish third, with the Linvilles eighth. That was in a dying breeze with our heavy-air Elvstrom sails up, so things looked good. We were second behind Peter Barrett the next day in a breeze, to take the series lead. The Linvilles were fourth in that race, but they won the next one with us second again. Our two seconds and a third were better than their first, fourth, and eighth, but they were closing.

The fourth race decided everything not because we won it and they finished third but because of the way that we won it. I made up my mind before the start that we would be right next to the Linvilles, just to see who was toughest. We started to leeward of them in moderate air, and soon we started going a little faster. They tacked, and we covered. We were headed in a puff and started to fall down on them a little, and I told Conn: "This is the series. Lean out there."

He did, and once again we started going a little better than they did. We both tacked several times toward the starboard tack layline, with them gaining in the tacks and us gaining in between, and finally we worked ourselves up to the layline, in first place with them in second just below us and able to fetch in second. Argyle Campbell was just behind and to windward of them in third.

I decided that this was the time to put the hammer to them, so I had Conn come in from the trapeze and we luffed our sails, waiting for the Linvilles to sail up into our wind shadow. When they were into our shadow, we got going again, sitting on them so badly that they could not fetch the mark. Campbell caught them to round second, and that's how we finished the race.

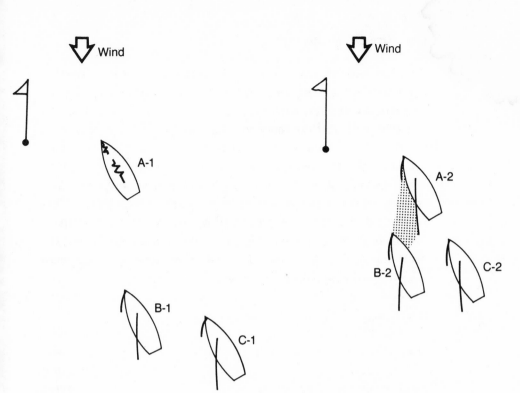

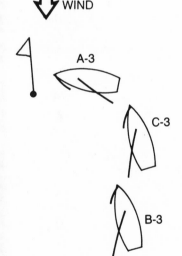

FIGURE 5. In a race in the 1976 Olympic Trials, Conner *(A)* luffed his sails and slowed up at the end of the first beat so he could blanket his main competition, the Linville brothers *(B)*. He slowed them down enough to let Argyle Campbell *(C)* in between them in second place. This all but clinched Conner's first place in the trials.

That was the last we saw of the Linvilles. By using this legal trick of driving one boat back to let another boat in, we seemed to discourage them, and they had two sevenths and a tenth in the last three races to finish only fourth for the series. Campbell was now the main threat, but we won the last two races to take the series by 10.3 Olympic points.

I was very pleased and somewhat surprised at winning the trials so easily, since it was only my sixth regatta in the class in ten months and we were sailing against people with as much as eight years of Tempest experience. The question now was whether we could continue to improve enough to win the gold medal at Kingston.

CHAPTER *12*

Bronze Medal
at Kingston

EVERY YEAR in the mid-1970s I went after the most important sailing event available. In 1974 it was the America's Cup,
in 1975 it was the Admiral's Cup, and in 1976 it was the Olympics. The yachting Olympic Games are the America's Cup of
small-boat racing, and it is no accident that both events are
now attracting the same group of world-class keelboat sailors:
Lowell North, Pelle Petterson, David Forbes, and John
Cuneo are Star and Dragon Class Olympic medalists who
have all been involved with American, Swedish, and Australian Cup contenders. The great Paul Elvstrom, a four-time
Olympic gold medalist, was for a while working with Baron
Bich on a French challenger. Buddy Melges, who is our best
one-design sailor, has twice turned down invitations to be
skipper or tactician of Twelves.

The quality of competition in the Olympics has improved
dramatically in the last ten years. This is partly because of the
financial support given to potential medal winners by most
countries. The United States provides some support, but no-

where near as much as did, say, Canada in 1976, with its two-hundred-thousand-dollar development program. Because of this support and because they enjoy sailing against each other, some of the very best sailors in the world end up in Olympic classes at one time or another.

Of my fifteen competitors at Kingston, I figured that Valentin Mankin was the one to beat. Mankin, from the Soviet Union, had won the gold medals in the Finn Class in 1968 and the Tempest in 1972. He had won the 1973 Tempest World Championship, yet had not sailed again in Western Europe until 1975. He had done poorly at the pre-Olympics at Kingston in 1975, but everybody knew that this master of tactical sailing would peak at the Olympics.

The second toughest sailor would be John Albrechtson, a Swede who had done well in Stars before picking up the Tempest. He was a close fourth at the Kiel Olympics in 1972, and he, his huge crew, Ingvan Hansson, and his Elvstrom sails had dominated the fresh-air pre-Olympics. He would be weak in light air, I thought, because as a sailmaker he was voluntarily restricted to his own product, which had been slow in that condition.

Two other threats were the 1974 and 1975 world champions, Uwe Mares (another ex-Star sailor), from West Germany, and Giuseppe Milone, from Italy. Also sailing were Felix Gancedo, a two-time Snipe world champion from Spain, Canada's Allen Leibel, against whom I had tuned the previous winter, and Allen Warren and Dave Hunt, the Britishers who had won the 1972 silver medal. With the exception of the latter, who were still using the same boat and rig they had in Germany, everybody had the hot combination of Mader hull, Proctor mast, and German North or Elvstrom sails.

With that kind of competition to anticipate, Conn and I were the first Tempest crew except for the Canadians to show up at the beautiful new three-million-dollar sailing center. The first race would be held July 19, and we were there on the fifth. I had asked the Linvilles to come up to Kingston and help me tune up, but they, understandably, said no. I then asked Argyle Campbell to help me tune up at Kingston, and he agreed. His help was invaluable. He loaned me his rudder to replace mine, which was not as good. At my request, the Olympic Committee chartered for Argyle's use Don Cohan's boat, which had shown great bursts of speed at the trials. At one stage I considered using that boat instead of my own, but we found after sailing every day that they were about the same speed and I preferred my own gear and layout.

We were allowed to measure in three suits of sails, and since my Elvstrom sails were getting a little tired and I could not get a duplicate suit in time, I acquired some new Norths. We still measured in the Elvstroms and used them in one or two fresh-air races, but otherwise we used German and United States Norths and a spinnaker made by Bruce Dyson, in Marblehead. Conn and Mark Reynolds (the son of my old Star crew and commodore of San Diego Yacht Club, Jim Reynolds) kept the boat up, and Carl Eichenlaub, who was the sailing team's maintenance man for the Games, reshaped the keel with microballoons to make it the same shape as the European keels. I felt pretty good about the boat and rig. Only Mankin's, which Mader had built in the Russian's presence, might have been a little stiffer and lighter in the ends. I think that my mast was one of the few at minimum weight. We were able to measure the hull, rig, and sails with no hitches whatsoever, mainly because the measuring at the Association Island trials had been so rigorous.

I wasn't sure whether I should worry about never having sailed at Kingston before. If you're new to an area, sometimes you can be more objective about it than somebody who has sailed there frequently. John Kolius, our Soling skipper who had beaten Buddy Melges in the trials, has sailed at Kingston at every August CORK regatta for six years, and he was very surprised when a northeast wind lasted for two races. Since I had never sailed there before, it didn't make any difference

to me that "it never blows from the northeast." I read a lot
of reports about wind at Kingston, and I listened carefully to
Rob Mairs, the United States team's excellent meteorologist.

After two weeks of worrying about all these problems, I
finally went racing. The first race was sailed in a moderate
on-shore breeze with a lumpy sea, and I went with Albrechtson, since I thought he was the one to beat in these conditions.
Mankin won, I was second and the Swede was fourth in a
straightforward race. Another second the next day in another
moderate-air race suddenly convinced me that we were actually going to win the gold medal. Mankin and Albrechtson
switched places, and I now led them both by a small margin.

But we were second after the third race, which left me
shaken and disappointed. The first leg was a disaster in which
I was first too greedy and then too conservative. Rob Mairs
had said in his pre-race weather briefing that the 6- to 12-knot
northeasterly would probably veer after the start, meaning
that we should go to the right. I went right, but I was surprised that none of the other leaders did. Once we were
headed, I should have consolidated my lead by tacking back
to the others, but we were soon lifted quite a bit, and the fleet,
to the left, looked pretty good. I decided to cut my losses,
tacked, and sailed up into the middle of the fleet—and then
the wind went right to leave us on the wrong side again. We
were ninth at the weather mark, leading only seven boats. I
had forgotten the rule about staying near your main competition. The closer you are to them, the less you will be affected
if there is a shift.

I was really depressed on this leg, but we caught two boats
on the reaches, two more on the next beat (by going left) and
one more, Mares, on the run to round the last mark fourth,
only thirty seconds behind the leader, Felix Gancedo. I tacked
right around the mark to go left, and Mankin, in third, tacked
to cover. We sailed almost all the way to the port tack layline,
gaining all the time, and when we both tacked to head toward
the finish it looked like we were narrowly ahead not only of

A Tempest start in one of the heavy-air races at Kingston with
Conner (US 318) looking good. *(Photo by John Rousmaniere.)*

the Russian but of Gancedo and second-place Albrechtson, who had gone right. As we neared the finish, those two went over to the left and Mankin and I held on port to the right. The two of us tacked and crossed Felix and John, leaving me with a very difficult problem. Should I cover Mankin or Albrechtson? Should I cover two boats or one boat? Thinking that Mankin was the man to beat, I continued to go left, and Gancedo and Albrechtson sailed right into a 10-degree header, tacked, and cleared both of us. What a frustrating end to the day. I had gone from ninth to fourth to first to third! As it turned out, if we had won that race we still would have lost the gold to Albrechtson, but who can say how our winning might have affected the remaining four races?

The next day was a flat calm for us, so the fourth race was sailed on July 23 in a southerly that started at about 12 knots and then died to 6 knots. We were third at the jibe mark, had a foul-up, and dropped to fifth, where we stayed. In almost every race, the same five boats made up a "first division"— Sweden, Russia, Italy, Germany, and us—and working up through those four boats was never easy. This was unlike the racing in the other keel class, the Soling, where going into the last race any one of seven boats could have won the gold medal.

Every series has a turning point. The turning point of the trials had been the end of the first leg of the fourth race, when we sat on the Linvilles and drove them back. The one of the Olympics for us was the third leg of the long, frustrating fifth race.

We sailed the long way out to the fifth start knowing we needed a good race because we were now pretty far behind Albrechtson. He had two firsts, a second, and a fourth for 10 Olympic points; we had two seconds, a third, and a fifth for 20.7. We had a worse throw-out race (six of seven races count in the Olympic system), but he had two firsts, which get bonus points. I decided that we had to get the best start, so I went for the favored pin end. "High risk, high reward," and we needed a high reward if we were going to win the one Olympic medal that really counts.

That start gave us an immediate two-boat-length lead in the dying off-shore northeasterly. We were quickly headed 10 and then 5 degrees, and suddenly we were in the lead, at least a hundred yards ahead of Albrechtson. The whole fleet tacked to port and we, up to windward, had more breeze and kept on gaining. I could see the other skippers sitting inside their boats while I was up on the windward rail. I looked up to windward, saw more wind, and tacked for it. We hit another big header, tacked almost on the layline and had a three-and-a-half-minute lead at the weather mark. We were so far ahead that we couldn't tell whose spinnaker was in second. We opened up a little more by the jibe mark—and then the wind dropped right out. The whole fleet caught up as did the Solings, which because of a general recall, had started half an hour after us. After two hours of near flat calm the thermal lake breeze finally filled in. The Flying Dutchmen, which started ten minutes ahead of us, the Tempests, and the Solings finished in a big pack. Even more deadly, we had dropped from the huge lead back to ninth, Albrechtson had climbed from eleventh to seventh, and Mankin went from ninth to second. We now had to count the fifth place, but even worse, I had to remember losing that enormous lead. It took the heart right out of me; it was the worst downer I have ever had in a sailboat.

We and about thirty-five other people protested the race on a variety of grounds. One was that all the calms and wind shifts had completely scrambled the required Olympic course of three beats, two reaches, and a run. Another was that a racing rule permits the jury to throw out races in which there are calms. Third, the reason that was good enough for me was that the race was a completely unfair test of sailing and did not belong in the Olympic Games.

The six-hour protest hearing was unique because we had so much opportunity to make our case. Normally you have

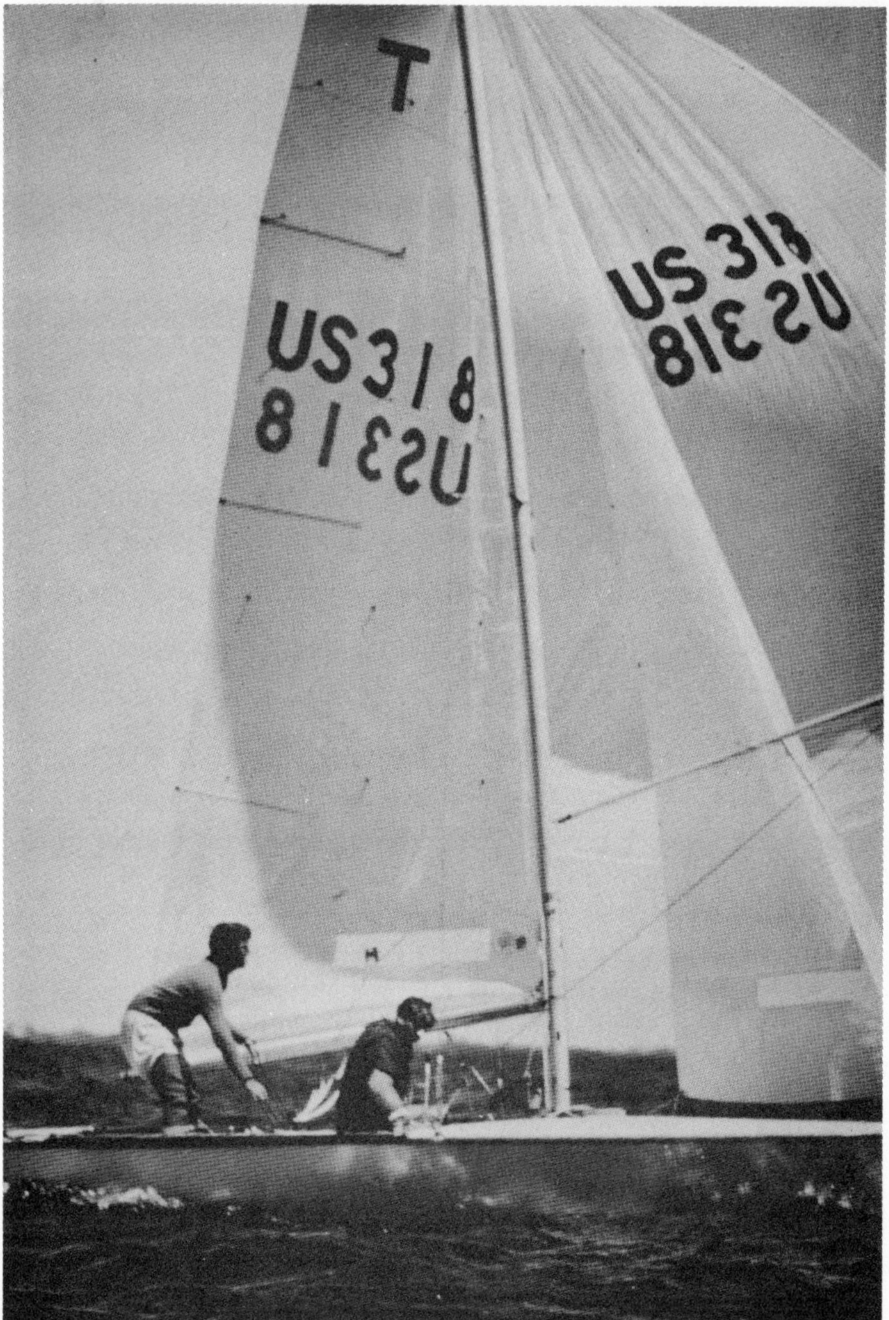
T
US 318
US 318
US 318
US 318

only two chances to argue—once when you make your defense and once when you comment on the other guy's defense. Then you leave and go sit at the bar and remember all the things that you should have said. But at this hearing there were so many people in the room that we all had plenty of time to think of something new after we made our initial statements. When I went into the room, I knew the race should be thrown out but that the jury would keep it in. After the hearing, I was so impressed by what I and the others had said that I was certain the jury, too, would want to throw the race out. Yet they debated for two hours and, with a divided vote, decided to count the race.

That all but eliminated my chance for the gold medal and now it was a fight for the silver with Mankin. The last two races were sailed in fresh air. We had a good start in the sixth and were moving well until the port trapeze wire broke part way up the first leg. I had to stop and help Conn back in the boat, and he sailed the rest of the race hanging off the trapeze handle by his arms on port tack. The wire, which was too small, had frayed just below the handle, and we should have spotted it and replaced it. Still, we finished fourth, one place behind Mankin. If we won the last race and Mankin finished worse than fourth, we had the silver. We led all the way around the course until Albrechtson caught us on the run, and although Mankin finished fifth, our second still left us 2.3 points behind him. Albrechtson's record was 4–1–2–1–2–1, he threw out his seventh in the fifth race and he won easily with 14 points. Mankin had 1–4–4–3–2–2, throwing out his last-race fifth, for 30.4 points. and my 2–2–3–5–4–2, throwing out the ninth, gave me 32.7 points. Mares was fourth, Milone was fifth, Gancedo was ninth, and the English, who were never in it with their old equipment, finished fourteenth. Two

Conner and his crew, Conn Findlay, in the fifth race at the Olympics. They were leading by almost four minutes at this stage, but shifts and a flat calm dropped them to ninth and out of serious contention for the gold medal. *(Photo by John Rousmaniere.)*

other Americans won medals—John Kolius, a silver in the Solings, and Dave McFaull, a silver in the Tornados.

I was very disappointed. Even the story about the English burning their old boat on the way in from the last race because they wanted to give it a dignified end did not cheer me up. Winning the bronze medal was a lot better than winning no medal at all, but losing a chance at the gold because of that terrible fifth race was depressing. I thought that I had sailed pretty well. Conn had done a perfect job crewing and in keeping up a strong, positive, and calm attitude. But our ability just wasn't enough, I'm afraid.

I was also very tired. It had been a busy seven months what with the SORC in *Charisma*, a Congressional Cup, racing and tuning Tempests in California, Florida, and Europe, and the Olympic Trials, not to speak of the intense two weeks leading into the Games themselves. There had been no time to rest and regroup my emotional resources. It was time to get back to my family and my work, to make some money to cover the huge expenses of buying and campaigning Tempests all around the world. Among my outlays had been about eight thousand dollars for each boat, expenses for six trips back and forth across the United States, travel costs to and in Europe, the value of sails and equipment, and salary for Mark Reynolds, who maintained the boats. I sold my Olympic boat immediately after the Games and then, after the Tempest was dropped from the Olympics in favor of the Star, I gave the other one to the University of Southern California.

In the meantime, I bought a good used Star, which, now that it was back in the Olympics, would again be the world's hot boat. Perhaps like Lowell North, who won the bronze medal in the Dragon in 1964 before winning the gold in the Star in 1968, I could come back a second time and win an Olympics. But that would have to wait. I raced only twice in

John Albrechtson and his huge crew, Ingvar Hansson, won the Olympic gold medal at Kingston in 1976. *(Photo by John Rousmaniere.)*

the last five months of 1976 as I recuperated from the early summer's sailing. The rest did me good, and by January, 1977, I was feeling good about racing again. Between races on the SORC in *High Roler*, I worked on my Star, and then got a third at the Spring Championship in New Orleans. In early summer, I easily won the North Americans at San Diego, with Ron Anderson crewing. Ron and I then went to the World Championship in Germany, where our speed was unbeatable and we won with a perfect record of first places. Winning my second Star Worlds almost made up for my disappointment at the Olympics, and I looked forward to more good racing in my favorite one-design boat.

V

"No Excuse to Lose"

CHAPTER 13

The Heavies—
North, Turner, Hood,
and Melges

I HAVE sailed with and against the best in 12-Meters, ocean racers, and small boats, and I think I have learned something from each person. What is interesting is that although each is especially good at one particular thing—leadership, boat preparation, helmsmanship—they all have this in common: when they get up in the morning and look at themselves in the mirror, they all have the self-confidence to be able to say realistically, "I'm the best."

When I was growing up in San Diego, I and everybody else knew that Paul Elvstrom was the best sailor in the world. A Danish sailmaker and boatbuilder, Elvstrom has won four Olympic gold medals, two Star World Championships, two Soling World Championships, a Half Ton World Championship, and lord knows how many other major championships in other classes. Business and health problems have kept him from racing much since the early 1970s, and it may be that he is burned out. But in the fifties and sixties, he was the god of yacht racing.

Lowell North, whom Conner calls the best all-round sailor in the world, goes over a piece of gear on the 12-Meter *Enterprise* with Rich du Moulin and John Marshall (back to camera). *(Photo by John Rousmaniere.)*

We all knew this, but we had trouble figuring out where Lowell North stood until somebody once decided that if Elvstrom was the god, Lowell must be the pope—which is why some of Lowell's friends and employees refer to him casually as "the Pope." I think that now Lowell must be the best all-round sailor in the world. I have lived near him all my life and have raced against him in Stars and with him in my ocean racers *Stinger* and *Carpetbagger*. I have come to know his strengths and weaknesses pretty well.

Lowell is a trained engineer now in his late forties who became interested in the technical side of sailing about twenty-five years ago. He started his own sail loft, which has since grown to a multi-million-dollar international organization of seventeen lofts. His early racing interest was in Stars, in which he has won an Olympic gold medal and four world championships. He also won the 1964 bronze medal in Dragons. In the early 1970s he became interested in ocean racing boats, particularly level-rating "Ton" boats, and he won the 1975 One Ton Worlds in *Pied Piper* and the 1976 SORC and Two Ton Worlds in *Williwaw*. He discovered about that time that he liked crewing, which enabled him to concentrate on all the details that keep racing through his mind without having to worry about steering. He crewed for Robbie Haines in a Soling in the 1976 Olympic Trials, and they finished second. When he was named skipper of the new Sparkman & Stephens 12-Meter *Enterprise*, he brought Malin Burnham aboard to steer upwind while he worked on tactics and sail trim. That he was dropped as skipper and *Enterprise* was not selected to defend does not change my mind about Lowell's ability.

Fascination with details is Lowell's strong point. Like myself, he probably does not think of himself as endowed with a great deal of natural sailing ability, but he and I both know that natural ability isn't everything. Practice, not natural ability, teaches you how to round a mark properly and how to trim a sail. Lowell is a fanatic about boat preparation and equipment. You always know that he will have lighter, more sophisticated gear than you will because he has put so much time and effort into doing things just right. For instance, with *Pied Piper* he was the first person to put a hydraulic cylinder on a headstay, to permit changing an ocean racing boat's balance by moving the top of the mast fore and aft. By letting the pump out, he could move the masthead aft and give the boat some necessary weather helm in light beating conditions. Then on a hard reach, he could shorten the headstay by pumping the cylinder up, moving the rig forward, and relieving the weather helm. When most people saw this, they thought it was dangerous and unseaworthy, even though it was rigged only on a small One Tonner. But by the next SORC, forty-foot Two Tonners had the gear and *High Roler*, my forty-six-footer, had one in 1977.

Though it's very hard to understand how anybody could beat Lowell on anything but talent in a small-boat race, he does have a weakness when it comes to big boats. He is a shy man who does not like to tell people what to do, so he may not have great leadership ability, which may have been his biggest problem on *Enterprise*. But he is changing as he becomes more confident in groups of people and as he gains ocean racing experience.

For contrast, take Ted Turner. By 1977, when he was thirty-seven, he had won two SORCs, a world ocean racing championship, and any number of distance races. He had done well in small boats, too, in 5.5-Meters and Flying Dutchmen, and he won the 1977 Congressional Cup match-racing series and the 1977 America's Cup. Ted's strong point is neither innate ability nor attention to detail and preparation— it is his enthusiastic competitiveness and leadership ability. He drives himself and his crew as hard as men can be pushed. This skill is really important in adversity, whether it is keeping *Mariner*'s crew together through the disastrous 1974 campaign, or driving *American Eagle* through two broken masts and any number of blown-out sails, or winning the 1977 America's Cup in an old boat, *Courageous*.

This combativeness can be good some of the time and bad some of the time. Ted has a tendency to think only of the battle and not the war. This may mean grinding down one opponent on a corner of a course while he forgets about the rest of the fleet. It may also mean steering for a dozen hours straight until he collapses with exhaustion. His kind of aggressive leadership works well when times are tough, but it can be counter-productive when things are going well. Ted did well early—winning his first SORC when he was twenty-six—because he sailed so much harder than anybody else. Of course, now that other people sail just as hard, it's more difficult for him to win.

Ted's charisma often leads people to underestimate his sailing ability. He is a good upwind helmsman, but he is one of the very best at downwind sailing. He seems to have a natural feel for driving off in puffs and heading up in lulls, and he has an excellent touch at choosing jibing angles and finding wind. His small-boat experience must help him here, but I know a lot of one-design sailors who don't have his feel downwind.

Ted Hood is very much like Lowell North in that he is an introvert and an extremely talented sailmaker and technical man. He is also limited as a leader. On one SORC he didn't even tell his crew where the boat would be docked. With a lot of people around he does very little talking. Sometimes instead of saying something, he will simply shrug his shoulders. In *Courageous*, I never did know if this shrug meant "no" and he didn't want to hurt my feelings by saying it, if it meant "yes," or if he didn't care. My approach to sailing is based on having a lot of quiet talk between the important people in the cockpit, but it just didn't seem to work with him.

Hood is in his late forties, like North, and is also an engineer. He was one of the first sailmakers to start working with

Ted Turner (left), about to make a speech, as usual. *(Photo by Bahamas News Bureau.)*

Dacron cloth back in the early 1950s, and he also invented the
cross cut spinnaker. His technical and business expertise in
sailing is enormous: he makes sailcloth, cuts sails, builds masts
and rigging, and designs and builds boats at his yard in Marblehead, Massachusetts. If there is a professional in sailing, he's
Ted Hood. He has made sails for most American 12-Meters and
has designed two of them, *Nefertiti* and *Independence*, unsuc-
cessful contenders in 1962 and 1977. As a sailor, he has won an
SORC, a Bermuda Race, and many ocean races in New England, where he is as much "the Pope" of sailing as Lowell is in
California. He was one of the first Americans to become interested in level racing, and he was sailing One Tonners in
Europe long before they become popular in North America.
And, of course, he won the America's Cup in 1974.

The following story says a lot about Ted Hood. In the 1974
SORC he was sailing one of his One Tonners, a boat that was
no better than anybody else's. Before the start of the St. Pe-
tersburg-Ft. Lauderdale Race, all the weathermen were pre-
dicting that the southerly would veer to the southwest. So we
in *Carpetbagger* and almost everybody else got on the port tack
after leaving Tampa Bay and footed for the header out into
the Gulf of Mexico. Instead of footing, Hood and Ted
Turner, in his One Tonner *Lightnin'*, stayed high. Each had
obviously decided that the other boat was the one to beat.
Turner gradually pulled away from *Robin Too II* (Hood names
all his own boats *Robin* or something derived from that name)
and Hood tacked. Turner, relying on the weather forecast,
kept on going on port and Hood, confident of his own experience and intuition, kept on going on starboard. The wind
backed to the east, *Robin Too II* finished one hour and three-
quarters ahead of *Lightnin'* and won the race, with Turner
tenth overall. Hood won the Circuit. Hood's self-confidence
also appeared when he disobeyed Bob McCullough's instructions to use a North mainsail in the first race of the 1974
America's Cup. That confidence may not be obvious when
you meet him, but it's there.

The 1977 America's Cup year began in 1976, when Ted Hood launched his *Independence*. Here he is seen during a December tune-up sail. *(Photo by John Rousmaniere.)*

It is not surprising that these three talented men—North, Turner, and Hood—were racing against each other in 12-Meters in the 1977 America's Cup summer, but there is one other man who is probably their superior in small boats. Buddy Melges grew up racing scows on the small lakes of Wisconsin, won three Mallory Cup North American sailing championships, took the bronze medal in the Flying Dutchman in 1964, and totally dominated the Soling fleet at the 1972 Olympics. Like North and Hood, he is a good technical man. He makes sails and builds boats, and is extremely talented with arrangements for sail-handling gear. Unlike them, he is a warm and outgoing man who deals well with people. I have never heard anybody say something bad about him. Melges exudes a positive attitude that is one of the reasons why he is so successful, along with hard work and obvious natural talent at steering a boat and at spotting wind shifts. Unfortunately, he has never chosen to prove himself in America's Cup, Congressional Cup, or offshore racing. This may be because his business is in small boats, but I think it may also be because he knows what kind of sailing he enjoys. If I were to have a sailing hero now, he would be Buddy Melges.

Lowell North, Ted Turner, Ted Hood, and Buddy Melges—they are the best sailors in North America and perhaps the world. But just a cut below them are a handful of other very talented men. One is Bill Buchan, a quiet, dedicated Seattle sailor who has won two Star Worlds, who does well in ocean racing, and who was tactician in *Intrepid* in 1974. Another—and an entirely different kind of person—is Tom Blackaller, a loud, aggressive, and charming guy from San Francisco who has won a Star Worlds and several international match-racing series in 6-Meters. In ocean racing, Dick Deaver and O.J. Young have to be considered in almost the same breath as North and Hood. Deaver is a sailmaker from Southern California who is particularly good at getting on an unfamiliar boat and making it go well. He did this in the 1976 One Ton Worlds and won. Young is a New Orleans boat yard owner

Buddy Melges. "If I were to have a sailing hero now, he would be Buddy Melges," says Conner. *(Photo by John Rousmaniere.)*

who has won an SORC, in *Muñequita* in 1973, and a Three-Quarter-Ton Worlds, in 1974 (with Deaver on board). They are both talented, competitive guys who attract loyal crews; and, though their technical ability may not be that of Hood or North, if you give them a good boat and good equipment, they will do well in any series.

The quality that links all of these sailors (and myself) is a winning self-image. They know they are the best men for the job of winning sailboat races, and most of them keep looking for more sailboat races to win. They have the self-confidence to know when to ask for help from experts and to know that playing the percentages is better than taking chances. They are talented, competitive men, but intelligent enough to realize that skill and drive are not enough. They have to work hard, too.

I think it all comes down to a statement: "Give yourself no excuse to lose." In the next chapter I will explain what that means to me.

CHAPTER 14

Why I Do It

AFTER EACH championship I've sailed, I've told myself, "This is the end," but somehow I find that I keep pushing myself to go on to the next big event, no matter what kind of boat it's sailed in. Here, I'd like to undergo some self-analysis and try to explain what makes Dennis sail.

First of all, I love competition, especially in sailboats. To me, a boat is to race. I simply do not like just to go sailing for enjoyment. For relaxation, I go to the mountains, but I don't go sailing. For me to take a daysail would be like Mario Andretti driving down to the grocery store after an Indianapolis 500. It's possible that my intense competitiveness stems from a childhood inferiority complex. I was not especially good looking, and I never really excelled at anything. Although I won a few high school letters in track, cross-country, and basketball, I was certainly not the star of the show. So when I found fairly early that I was pretty good at sailing, I worked hard at it because, I think, I was trying to prove to myself that I really could be successful after all. I enjoyed those brief pats on the back that come when you're good at something. Sailboat racing became the outlet for my desire to excel, and helped overcome some of my feelings of inferiority. It showed me that I *could* be one of the best at something.

I think the high point of my sailing career came in 1971, before I became so involved with international big-boat racing. That was when I won my first Star Worlds at age twenty-eight. That is the pinnacle of my yachting life. My motivation to excel and my satisfaction at winning have decreased since then, with every success. This isn't unique to me. I'm sure that Lowell North and Buddy Melges have discovered the same thing. At one time or another, each proved to himself that he was the best, and after he proved that to himself there was less and less need to prove it to the public. Other factors, such as patience, experience, and self-confidence, may compensate for this decrease in ambition, so the more experienced sailor may not need to expend a lot of energy if only because he knows what the priorities are.

But right now, I really do love the competition, whether in a Sabot or in a 12-Meter. I enjoy the logistics and organization, but what I love most of all is doing well. When I'm winning sailboat races I'm more at peace with myself and less pushy. Someday, I may be able to stop trying to prove something to myself and the world, but I don't think I'm there yet, psychologically. Winning sailboat races is a way of life to me now, but my life is gradually changing and my job and family are becoming more important. Of course I can't simply say, "Sailing isn't important to me any more." I've sailed something like four or five hours a day for fifteen years, and unless I were suddenly to get involved with another activity, I couldn't just change that habit. One problem with this attitude is, now that I think I'm pretty good, I find it very hard to *not* win. A lot of people congratulated me for winning the bronze medal in the Olympics, but I know I should have won the silver and, if I'd worked a little harder and longer, I might have won the gold. Doing well, I have expectations of myself that are hard to satisfy. How would Bruce Jenner have felt if he had finished third in the decathalon? That's how I felt.

I think that we all have an interior "comfort zone," a psychological state that we want to be in. Picture a good club golfer who is playing Jack Nicklaus. His self-image is probably that he is a good golfer, but not good enough to beat Nicklaus, so he will be more comfortable losing than winning. If he beat Nicklaus, he would be uncomfortable with the demands of his new self-image so he does whatever he can to get back in that comfort zone, even if it means missing a two-foot putt on the eighteenth green. If his self-image included beating Jack Nicklaus, he could make that putt.

In sailing, an average sailor who gets ahead of Lowell North or Buddy Melges or Dennis Conner in an important series will most likely do something dumb or careless in order to get behind. But once he gets behind he'll stick like glue and not lose another foot. You see people like this in every fleet. They are very hard to beat at the local level, but once at a major championship their blazing boat speed disappears because they simply can't picture themselves winning that worlds or nationals.

In 1971, my personal goal was simply to qualify for the Star Worlds, and my self-image was that of a person who sailed in the worlds but who did not win it. I had been a skipper for only a year, this was my first year in the Stars, and my boat was four years old, so winning a Star World Championship seemed out of reach. To somebody growing up in San Diego, the Star Class had the greatest sailing and sailors there were, and since many of those sailors lived in San Diego, just qualifying for the worlds through the local district took some doing.

But when I amazed myself by finishing a close second in the district eliminations, my self-image started to change. Having qualified, I set myself the goal of being in the top ten at the worlds. I honestly didn't feel that I could win. But when I *did* win, my self-image changed a whole lot. For all those years a Star World Championship had signified the best sailor in the world and now, all of a sudden, I was a Star world champion. My image of a Star champion was of somebody who very rarely lost any races at all, anywhere, so all of a sudden that image became my self-image, and my comfort zone changed radically. Now I could no longer take a casual approach to racing, because, since I was a Star world champion, I had to be serious and win all the time.

From then on, I couldn't give myself any excuses to lose. There are some sailors who don't work hard on their boats and gear, and I think it's because they are looking for excuses to lose. They may blow a series when a piece of gear breaks, or their sails or keel may not be just right. They can always blame a loss on their equipment. It may be that those guys really *want* to lose. But somebody like Lowell North or myself will be comfortable with himself only if he works hard on his equipment. A guy content with a third because he can say that the top two crews won only because they worked harder is also comfortable with himself. His self-image is that of a person who could be the best in the world "if only."

Once you get to the point when you honestly feel inside that you have done everything within your power to win and have given yourself no excuse to lose, you're really going to be hard to beat. You'll buy the same boats and sails that everybody else does and you won't use radical tactics or equipment, but you will do a lot more work and you'll know you're at least as good as everybody else. Putting this much energy and time into sailboat racing takes its toll. First of all, boats are not cheap. I bought two Tempests and spent a lot of money on gear and travel to prepare for the Olympics, perhaps about twenty-five thousand dollars in all—and the Tempest is much smaller and cheaper than *High Roler* or even *Stinger*. I work very hard when I'm not sailing to put money aside for the future, because I think it's going to be a lot harder to become wealthy in ten years than it is now. Yet I still devote a lot of time and money to an activity that many people would call a luxury. It is very rewarding to the ego to be on top of a field, and I have a big ego. From time to time I develop very good intentions of quitting sailing, but whenever I do that, another challenging opportunity seems to come along. It's almost as though I'm addicted to the competition. But other things draw me back. I like the people, especially the real sailors. Sailors as a group are great. And being from California, I've always had the feeling that I had something to prove in the east. When I started going to the SORC, I ran into people who thought that California was just a place where a bunch of hippies lived. They didn't realize there were any sailors in California. West Coast sailors won the SORC in 1975, 1976, and 1977, and in 1977 all three classes in the division for new boats were won by West Coast boats. Now that West Coast sailors have done so well in other major international events—for instance, Bill Ficker and I, both from Southern California, steered the winning boats in the 1970 and 1974 America's Cups—we have less to prove, and in our own minds we enjoy parity with East Coast sailors.

I think that my amateur status gives me a little extra motivation to do well in a sport dominated by professionals like sailmakers. There's no question about it, some of the very best sailors are professionals—Lowell North, Buddy Melges, Ted Hood, Dick Deaver. Some people have suggested that the professionals should sail by themselves, but if they did, racing certainly wouldn't be fun for me any more. Then I would *have* to be a sailmaker or a boat builder if I wanted to sail against top competition. Certainly, the amateurs would start to win races again, but there is no way that they could fool themselves into thinking that they were the best. In a way, there already are professional and amateur leagues. If you want to race against the professionals, go buy yourself a Soling or a One Tonner. If you want to race with the amateurs, buy yourself a Catalina 27 or a Thistle.

As for my own sailing, now that the Star boat is back as

The victor and his spoils after the 1975 SORC. *(Photo by Bahamas News Bureau.)*

an Olympic Class, I think I'll work hard at winning a gold medal in the 1980 games, although if I have the opportunity to sail in the America's Cup that year, I may have to change my mind. The Cup is still the greatest thrill in sailing. I enjoy ocean racing and will keep at it, if my financial situation doesn't change. But I like racing little boats, especially Stars, so much that I'm sure I'll emphasize them; also, I will continue to like match racing. Its demands are different than those of other kinds of racing. There is less preparation, but there is more demanded of the skipper's skills and physical ability, and of his confidence. I know I'm good at all those kinds of sailing, and I am challenged by them. Yet I have done everything in boats I have ever dreamt of doing, so what can I do next? About the only goals I can set for myself are, like Lowell North, to win an Olympic gold medal and to win two more Star World Championships, and to be skipper of a 12-Meter in the America's Cup. I think those are realistic goals, since my abilities are not decreasing. A sailor has reached his peak when his reflexes, sight, and drive begin to fade at about age forty-five, and I've got over ten years to go. If sailing continues to be a high enough priority, you keep getting better until your late forties.

And I'm sure it will continue to be a high enough priority for me.

Index

Adams, Billy, 43
Admiral's Cup Races, 97, 102, 104, 109–10, 112
  1975, 105–13, 157
  1977, 115, 125
aggressor versus defender, 28, 30, 34, 36
Albrechtson, John, 132, 135, 153, 158, 160–63, 165–67
Allen, Tom, 19–20, 22, 140
aluminum, use of, 49, 87
American Eagle, 41, 48, 174
America's Cup Races, 27, 31, 40, 42–43, 55, 59, 62, 66, 69–70, 79, 179, 188
  1964, 48, 56
  1967, 49
  1970, 42, 49, 58, 67, 73, 186
  1974, 17, 33–34, 36, 39, 42, 55, 62, 66, 73, 78–80, 85, 157, 177, 186
  1977, 16, 51, 60, 79–80, 125, 127, 174–75, 178–79
  1980, 188
Anclote Key Races, 96–97, 118
Anderson, Ron, 168
Anderson, Stu, 19, 134–35
Andron, Jon, 16, 91

Barrett, Peter, 84, 138, 154
Barton, Bob, 99
Bavier, Bob, 48, 53, 56–59, 62, 79
Bay Bea, 115, 118–19, 123, 125
Bennett, Pete, 133
Bich, Baron, 157
Blackaller, Tom, 179
boats, selection of, 131–32
Boca Grande Races, 118, 120
Bond, Alan, 66, 72–73, 76, 78
Bootlegger, 95, 97–101
Bown, Ashley, 17–19

Boyd, Richie, 43
Buchan, Bill, 25–27, 59, 64, 147, 179
Bumblebee 3, 111–12
Burnham, Malin, 17–18, 22–23, 125, 173
Burns, Bob, 91

Cal 40s, 27–29, 34, 41
Caldwell, Bud, 17
Calkins, Skip, 84
Campbell, Argyle, 148, 150–52, 154–55, 159
Carousel, 17–18
Carpetbagger, 84, 91–92, 173, 177
Catalina 27s, 186
Chance, Brit, 41–50, 115
Charisma, 98, 100, 102, 104–6, 109–14, 118, 123, 131, 149, 166
cleats, 134, 152
Cohan, Don, 150, 153, 159
compasses, 138–39, 141
Congressional Cup Races, 27–28, 31, 41, 50, 150, 179
  1971, 27
  1972, 27
  1973, 27
  1974, 27
  1975, 27–29, 149
  1976, 28, 30
  1977, 28, 174
Constellation, 48
Country Woman, 98–101
Courageous, 28, 33–34, 46–69, 73–78, 125, 127, 131, 175
crew, choice of, 134–35
Croce, Bebbe, 73
Cuneo, John, 67, 157
currents, 106, 141

Dayton, Duke, 42
Dean, Peter, 148
Deaver, Dick, 31, 83, 93, 95, 97, 99, 101, 115, 179, 181, 186
deck layout, 62, 88–90
depth sounders, 19
Derecktor, Bob, 41, 43, 45
Doyle, Robbie, 39, 43–45, 52
Dragon (class), 67, 157, 166, 173
Driscoll, Gerald, 16–17, 19, 49, 58–59, 63–64
du Moulin, Rich, 39, 43, 47, 49, 172
Dyson, Bruce, 159

Edgecomb, L.J., 72, 106
Eichenlaub, Carl, 17, 19–21, 84–87, 114–15, 159
Elvstrom, Paul, 157, 171, 173
Enterprise, 16–17, 125, 127, 172–74
Ericson 39s, 92
Escort, 68–69
European Championships, 150–51

faking a tack, 30, 32
favored side of course, 31, 34–36
Ficker, Bill, 42, 49, 58, 186
Findlay, Conn, 43, 141, 148–54, 158–59, 165
Finn (class), 147, 158
Fisher, Matt, 141–44
Flying Dutchman (dinghy) (class), 41, 147, 163, 174, 179
Forbes, David, 157
Fort Lauderdale Races, 96–100, 118–20
Foster, Glen, 148
fouling, 73–76
470 (class), 147
France, 67
Frazee, Nick, 87
Fredericks, Doug, 43
Frers, German, 118–19
Frers 46s, 119, 123

Ganbare, 84–85, 87
Gancedo, Felix, 158, 160–62, 165
Gleich, Marty, 21, 83
Goldsmith, Bruce, 142–44
Gretel II, 67, 73, 125

Haggerty, Pat, 115
Haines, Robbie, 173
Hallelujah, 83
handicaps, 85
Hansson, Ingvar, 135, 158, 166–67
Hardy, Jim, 67, 72–74, 76
headings, 139
Helfrich, Bunky, 43
Herreshoff, Halsey, 59, 63–64, 68, 71, 106, 111
High Roler, 43, 85, 88–91, 109, 114–27, 168, 174, 185
Hinman, George, 40–43, 46–48, 50–52
Holt, Allen, 27, 135
Hood, Ted, 39, 45, 56–64, 67–73, 78–80, 93–94, 104, 110–12, 119, 125, 171–81, 186
Howard, David, 43
hulls, 132–33, 150–52

Hunt, Dave, 158
"hunting down," 31

Imp, 125
Independence, 60, 125, 177
Inflation, 101
International Yacht Racing Union, 73
Intrepid, 17, 42, 48–50, 53, 55–59, 62–64, 67–68, 73, 125, 179

jibing, 30, 32–36, 64, 70, 93–94, 140
jib leads, 94–95, 134, 149

Kialoa II, 18–19
Kialoa III, 95, 99, 118
Kilroy, John, 18–19, 95
Kingfish, 87
Kirsch, Chuck, 118
Knapp, Arthur, 145
Kolius, John, 147, 159, 166

Lawson, Peter, 106, 111
laylines, 31, 33–34, 71, 154, 160, 163
Leibel, Allen, 148, 158
level racing, 85
Lewis, Kip, 110–11
Lightnin', 41, 177
Lightning (class), 19–22, 131, 140, 147
Lightning World Championships, 141
  1965, 22
Lipton Cup Races, 96, 100–1, 112, 119, 121, 123
Linville, Jack and Jim, 148, 150–52, 154–56, 159, 162
Liracas, Steve, 106
Long Beach Yacht Club, 27
luffing, 30, 33, 70, 140, 155

McComb, David, 148
McCullough, Bob, 55–59, 62, 68–69, 79–80, 177
McFaull, Dave, 166
Mairs, Rob, 160
Mallory Cup Races, 179
Mankin, Valentin, 132, 139, 158–60, 162–63, 165
Mares, Uwe, 158–59, 165
Mariner, 27, 39–58, 78, 102, 148, 174
Marshall, John, 67–69, 172
match racing, 27–28, 30–35, 72, 93
Melges, Buddy, 134, 147, 157, 159, 171–81, 183–84, 186
Merchant Marine Academy, 42
Miami to Nassau Races, 91, 96, 101, 113, 122–23
Miller, Bob, 67
Miller, Dave, 91
Milone, Giuseppe, 158, 165
Mitchell, Ben, 91–93, 99, 101, 114
Moody Blue, 93
Morgan, Henry, 55, 64
Mosbacher, Bus, 49
Mueller, Jack, 85, 87
Mull, Gary, 84, 88
Muñequita, 181

Nassau Cup Races, 96, 101–2, 122–23
navigation, 18, 72, 76, 88, 90
Nefertiti, 177